# Perspectives

### Arthur C. Nordin

Peppermill Press
Hockessin, Delaware

## Arthur C. Nordin

Arthur C. Nordin (Art) was born in 1916 to Swedish parents, who separately immigrated from Sweden and met in the United States. He grew up in the shore town of Asbury Park, New Jersey. At that time, Asbury Park was a retreat area for wealthy New Yorkers. His father left when he was 10. He had no idea what happened to his father until well after he was married and saw his father's name in a Swedish newspaper. After the death of his mother, Art and his wife, Dorothy, traveled to Bridgeport, Connecticut to be reunited with his father.

Being a single parent in the 20's and 30's was not easy. Art's mother survived by renting rooms to wealthy visitors. From an early age, Art worked: he rode his bicycle and sold ice cream, candy, and newspapers to help his mother make ends meet. In his teen years, he got a job greasing pans at a local bakery. He had no hope of a higher education until The King's College (founded by evangelist Percy Crawford) opened nearby.

Art was a member of The King's College first class. He continued working at the bakery at night and attending school during the day. During the Second World War, the government bought the college property. They relocated to northern Delaware. Art made a huge decision to give up steady work at the bakery and move to Delaware. After years of struggling to pay his tuition, Art graduated in 1946 with a teaching degree.

Teaching jobs were scarce, so he worked in a ship building yard and as a brick layer during the war. He eventually got a position teaching at the Ferris School for Boys in Wilmington, Delaware. This enabled him to get his foot in the door so he could eventually teach in the public-school system. Art taught math, elementary science, and music for 25 years.

Art and Dorothy had two children, Sherri and Eric. After Dorothy's death, Art married Gerry, who had a daughter, Susy. They shared 31 years together.

Following Art's retirement in 1980, he took many trips – both in the United States and abroad. Art spent his adult life studying the Bible, playing the piano and teaching. He always told others about their need for a relationship with Jesus. In 1991, he received a cancer scare and decided it was time to become completely dedicated to the Lord. It was then he began writing Christian articles.

For the remainder of his life, he developed quite a mailing list and, eventually, an email list. He went home to be with the Lord in 2011. This book is a compilation of some of Art's most powerful essays.

*To God Be the Glory Forever!*

# Table of Contents

# Perspectives

By Arthur C. Nordin

Edited by Gerry Nordin, Emily Piraino
& Karen Randall

# 7' X 10'

In a 7' X 10' cell, a man must spend the rest of his life. He murdered his girlfriend, was convicted, and sentenced, first to be executed, and later, to life without parole.

The man had a successful career as a lawyer, was a multimillionaire, and enjoyed the good life. The main comments on the case that I heard and read in the paper were solely about the tragedy of his loss of the good life. "He could be sailing the Caribbean in his private yacht, feasting on the finest foods, and taking in the best entertainment, but now he's locked up in that tiny cell forever." My thought on the case is the exact opposite. How fortunate he was to be spared the death penalty, giving him time to reconsider his choices and make new ones. Whereas he had been a slave to the worldly life, which leads to eternal death, he is now freed from it, never to be bothered with it again. Where he had no time for God, not even a minute, he now has 24/7 to seek the wisdom that comes only from above. Where his former life would have landed him in the torment of hell forever, he now can become one of God's overcomers, according to Revelation 2:26, rising to the highest heights of glory and honor. You see, in prison he not only has the privilege of being free from all distractions, but he also has the time to write down what he learns and share it with the world. If this seems far out, consider the Apostle Paul. He was put in jail on a trumped-up charge and wrote letters that are still cherished by millions 2000 years later. Martin Luther was locked up and translated the Bible from Latin to the language of the people, changing the world forever. David, one of God's all-time favorites, was a murderer and a thief. He not only stole a man's wife, but he also had the man murdered. In spite of this abomination, David's greatest obsession was to love the Lord. He was called the sweet psalmist of Israel, having written so many of the Psalms. He was called 'a man after God's own heart,' because he always put God first. He rose to be the greatest king that ever lived.

This tremendous opportunity and privilege has been handed to this man on a platter. What will he choose - a life of bitterness, or a life of service and glory? If he makes a bad choice this time, he'll be wishing for all eternity that he could get to that 7'x10' cell.

## A Checkered Life

A friend of mine said, "You sure have had a checkered career, haven't you?" This was after I mentioned some vicissitude I went through during my early years. I wasn't sure if this was a compliment or what, so I looked it up. It means alternating between good and evil fortunes, the ups and downs of life. I had never thought of my life that way, so I decided to look back and see how up and down it was. One thing I knew without looking, it wasn't a walk in the park!

The beginnings were good, all uppers. My father had a delicatessen in Sea Bright, N.J. Delicatessen means choice or delicious eating. I still remember going behind the counter for samples. The store was on Ocean Avenue, so the beach was my playground. When I was about six, mother's mother became ill and we had to make a quick trip to Sweden. It turned out to be a whole year, one of the best years of my life. Imagine a kid being on an ocean liner for two weeks, then seeing land again, meeting relatives, going to the land of the midnight sun, going to the new airfields, and learning a new language. When we came back to the U.S., I had forgotten the English language! Back in Sea Bright, a downer was on the way. My parents split up. I was partly to blame, because I ran across Ocean Avenue and was nearly killed. Mother refused to live there anymore, and moved to Asbury Park, N.J. Overnight I lost everything: my father, the beach, the playground, the store, the big house, the canal a block away, and the boats, etc. We now lived in a little apartment on Main Street - not much safer than Ocean Avenue.

Then suddenly things were on the upswing. My parents were together again and bought a new house in Asbury Park. That was one of the best times of my life, a real upper. Asbury Park was the most beautiful town in New Jersey, bounded by the ocean, lakes and sand dunes. The boardwalk had every amusement, including a merry-go-round, Ferris wheel, roller coaster, penny arcade, canoes, and rowboats, etc. The block we lived on was the best in the city. Every house had kids my age; there was never a dull moment. In the summer, everything was in full swing. In my teens, the best thing of all was the casino, where big name bands, like Tommy Dorsey, came. Those years couldn't have been better. But another downer was on the way.

My parents split up again, this time for good. On top of that, the depression came, and we lost our house and moved to a flat. As bad as that was, it led to something better. Mother had a wonderful idea. She had a lot of furniture, so why not rent a big house near the ocean and rent rooms. She did this, and it became a big upper, getting us through the depression, plus affording us the pleasure of meeting interesting people. We even had the Mayor of Trenton as a guest, but a downer was waiting.

I graduated from high school and couldn't find a job. I finally got one in a bakery greasing pans at 40 cents an hour. I thought it was okay, since some of my friends were only making 25 cents an hour. By this time, I had a girlfriend who promised me true love. I quickly called her with the good news of my job. She said, "Oh, darling, I'm so sorry. I just got engaged." I went down to the basement, where nobody would see me, and did some heavy thinking. In a couple months, the bakery business slowed down and they said, "Sorry, old pal, we won't need you until summer." Down to the basement again. In the middle of winter, they called me back. One of the workers had gotten hurt. I had my eyes on a car now. Two months later, the injured man was back on the job and I had to forget the car. Eventually, I was rehired, and four years went by. I was still making 40cents an hour. Relatives of the owners started out at $1.00 an hour, and they had plenty of relatives. Then I ran into some of my friends who had gone to college. They were now graduates who were making real money, driving new cars, and dating the beauty queens. That was one of the lowest ebbs of my life, and there wasn't any hope in sight.

Suddenly, the sky became a little brighter. I didn't realize then how bright it would become. The King's College, a Christian college, opened nearby. By working the night shift, I could go to school and make enough to pay the bills. It would be a tough row to hoe, but it was worth a try, so I signed up. One consequence that never occurred to me was my mother's thoughts on the subject. She said, if I planned to live at the college, she would give up housekeeping and go to New York. I didn't realize it at the time, but that made me a homeless person. I didn't feel it until Christmas vacation came and everyone went home but me. To top it off, they said I could stay at the school, but they didn't tell me the heat would be turned off! Oh well, the arrangement worked well for three years. My days started at 2 in the morning, being in class by 10, taking a nap in biology class (when possible), and being in bed at 8. It was a grind.

Two super summers occurred by accident. Percy Crawford, the founder of the college, suddenly needed a lifeguard for his camp in the Poconos and asked if I was interested. Was I! How I got away from the bakery is another story. Later, the traveling gospel team lost their piano player and asked me to fill in. The third year ended with the announcement that The King's College was moving to Delaware. Consternation! What was I to do? Jobs were still scarce. If I quit the bakery and couldn't get a job in Delaware, I'd really be in trouble. Fortunately, or providentially, after three years of Christian teaching, I was a firm believer and could cast my burden on the Lord. By September, I got the impression, intuition, or whatever, that I should make the move.

That fall in Delaware, the best job I could find was two days a week in an A&P at 50 cents an hour. I could see the writing on the wall. Sure enough, by April, the college posted a notice on the bulletin board, "Pay your bills." I was broke, so I quit. Looking back, I'm amazed that nobody offered to arrange for me to pay later. It didn't happen, so all my hopes were dashed. It was basement time again.

I rented a room at the YMCA in Wilmington and started looking for a job. I found one right away at 77 cents an hour. I couldn't believe it. I soon found out why. It was the spring of '41 and war clouds were darkening. Suddenly, there were jobs everywhere. There was also the Army, Navy, and Air Force. I decided to go for the Air Force. They required two years of college, so I was in. A week later they informed me that since the college was not accredited; they couldn't accept me. Back to square one. The shipyards were now hiring, and I became a painter, working at night and going to a seminary during the day. Then I was drafted, and surprise, surprise, they told me to stay in school. They needed chaplains. I didn't know if that was an upper or downer, since the country was super patriotic, and everyone was supposed to be "in the service." I kept working and studying, and finally had my degree. I was beginning to see a little light at the end of the tunnel. By now, my mother was back from New York and living with me, I had a little money in the bank, a car, and a girlfriend. I warned her that I had three P's that could cause problems: I was Poor, had a Parent living with me, and was Pentecostal. She said she was the right one for me, and I was the right one for her. I popped the question and she said, "Yes." Everything was wonderful, but there was one nagging thought. She was in Asbury Park and had never seen Wilmington. Shouldn't she, at least, come and have a look? To make a long story short, she came, she saw, and she changed her mind. This was after my hometown newspaper had announced the engagement with a big picture, and after I had made a big sacrifice to buy a diamond ring for nearly $400. The pay scale back then was $1.00 an hour, so figure that out. What happened to the ring, I'll never know. That, again, seemed like the lowest ebb of my life, or at least one of them. I didn't have a basement at the time to do the heavy thinking, but it was Romans 8:28 that got me through it.

Finally, the war was over the shipyard closed, and ten thousand people were looking for jobs. I now had two degrees and was qualified to teach. Surprise, surprise, everywhere I went, it was the same story, "Teachers are a dime a dozen." It was back to square one again. Nevertheless, the Lord helped me. I found a job at the Railway Express Agency taking big parcels from the railroad cars, loading them on a truck, and delivering them. It was a job, but the pay was low. All I could do was cry, "Oh, Lord, remember me. I'm still in trouble."

Right about then, the Lord sent me a real treat to boost my spirits. Someone told me the Quakers were sending relief supplies, including cattle, to Germany and they needed chaplains. I applied and was hired. Going abroad was something I had dreamed about but never thought would happen. While in Bremen, the captain of the ship next to us came over and said he needed six seamen. His ship was sailing all around the world. I sweated that out all night. Imagine having a dream like that dropped in your lap! But I had responsibilities back home, so I told him I just couldn't do it. That was a high and a low at the same time!

Back in the U.S., a huge building boom of hundreds of homes was under way. I hurried over, and became a plasterer, third class, at $1.25 an hour. That was an upper. A few weeks later, I said to myself, "This job is not for me." Next, I watched the block layers and thought they had it better. I became a block layer, third class. A few weeks later, I said to myself, "You'll never be a block layer." Next, I watched the bricklayers. That looked easy enough. Praise the Lord; at last I had something that was tolerable. As soon as I saw that I was as speedy as the rest of them, I asked for a raise. They said, "Can you do a fireplace?" They had me on that. I went to another contractor, then another. To make a long story short, it took me a couple years, but I became a master craftsman. By this time, I had money in the bank, a car, a new girlfriend, and was ready to pop the question. I still had the three Ps to consider. She knew about them, but I wanted to make it perfectly clear (Nixon's famous line) that they were part of the package. She said, "No problem," to each one.

I could hardly believe it. So, the die was cast. Dorothy and I were soon on our way to New Orleans for our honeymoon. I was all of 34 years old. The Lord had put me through the mill with all the ups and downs, but it seemed like it would be clear sailing now, for a while, at least. We were both making good money and saving for a house. Everything was good. Jobs were everywhere. My biggest job was building a gym for The King's College. I don't know where I got the nerve to tackle such a building, but it came out right. I was ready to point to it with pride, when The King's College moved to New York. Getty Oil, the new owners of the property, tore the gym down!

Despite the good times, a question kept nagging me. It was about my being a bricklayer. It was an honorable job, good money, and I enjoyed it, but was that what God wanted me to do? I said, "Lord, there is something wrong with this picture. I paid dearly for an education. Was it all for nothing?" Soon after that, several good things happened. First, I saw a notice on the job bulletin board about a class for estimating and blueprint reading. I took that and immediately got a job teaching it at night. A year or two later, Ferris School for Boys asked me to teach 8th grade. A year later, the principal died, and they asked me to be the principal. A year after that, the Red Clay School District offered me a job teaching 6th grade science. At last, I felt like I was out of the tunnel. Anyone reading this would have to agree that it was a mighty checkered life, but when you get where you're going and are satisfied that the Lord led you all the way, it's a mighty good feeling. I stayed on that job for 25 years and never had a bad day. During this time, my wife and I were blessed with two wonderful children, Sherri and Eric. We took trips everywhere and had long vacations (school-teacher summers). Twenty-eight years later, my dear wife, Dorothy, went home to be with the Lord. It was a real downer, but the Lord blessed me with a second wife, Gerry, who also brought a daughter, Susy, into our marriage. At the time of this writing, I have had 27 years of retirement that couldn't be beat. P.T.L.

In retrospect, I'd say uppers and downers are a good thing. Seeing how God rescues us from hopeless situations is a cause for much thanksgiving. It is also the only way to empathize with people going through tough times. Think of how great it will be when we get to heaven and look at God's DVDs of our times on earth and laugh at the many times; we thought our world was crashing!

A chorus that helped me through the tough times follows:

> He is just the one to meet my every need.
> He has proved Himself a friend to me indeed.
> To my problems, whether great or small,
> Jesus is the answer, so on Him I call.
> He is just the one to meet my every need.

As I end my story, I must make it perfectly clear that all the strivings to get up and stay up, though important, were not the ruling principle of my life. Success or failure in this life cannot be compared with success or failure in the Spiritual life. The keyword for this life is temporary. Someone said, "Only one life, 'twill soon be past, only what's done for Christ, will last." I believe many broom pushers will outshine CEOs on the day of judgment. We will either hear, "Well done," from the Master or "Depart from me." May this soliloquy be of some help to those who are on the roller coaster period of their lives.

## A Well or a River

Jesus said, "*The water I shall give shall be a well of water springing up into everlasting life.*" (John 4:14) In John 7:38, Jesus said, "*He that believes in Me - out of his innermost being shall flow rivers of living water. This He spoke of the Spirit, which they that believe on Him should receive.*" These two verses are talking about the Holy Spirit.

There are two types of wells: the kind that need priming and pumping, and the artesian well that flows without pumping. We have three types of flowing water: a pump well, a flowing well, and a river. Bear in mind, the water is the Holy Spirit. Isaiah 12:3 says, "*With joy shall you draw water out of the wells of salvation."* 2 Peter 2:17 also speaks of wells without water. Here we have two kinds of people: a good Christian that is sharing his faith with others and doing it with joy, and a nominal Christian (in name only) who doesn't share because he has nothing to offer. This nominal Christian is a well without water. Stop to ask yourself, "Is that good Christian a picture of me?"

Then we come to the river of water. This speaks of an overflowing of the Holy Spirit. This is not a Christian that reads a few Bible verses once in a while and spends three or four minutes in prayer occasionally. Rather, he is pictured in Romans 5:5: *"The love of God, by the Holy Ghost, is shed abroad in our hearts."* Everywhere he goes, people detect there is something different about him. Paul describing it in 2 Corinthians 2:15 says, *"We are unto God a sweet aroma of Christ, in them that are saved and in them that perish - life to life, and death to death."*

In Acts 8:1, there was a great persecution against the church. They were all scattered but they preached the Word everywhere they went (Verse 4). You might think this is speaking of preachers, not so. The first church was not divided into clergy and laity. Everybody preached and thousands were converted. This was the river of life that Jesus was talking about, that overflowed its banks and changed the world. It turned it upside down! (Acts 17:6) This is what the world needs today, but to all appearances, the river has dried up.

The state of the church today is far from that of the early church. We read in Genesis 26:18 about Isaac's wells where it explains that the Philistines had stopped them up. Philistines are, of course, Satan's emissaries who are just as busy in our day and age stopping up the river of life. Isaac didn't give up, and in verse 19 he dug another well of springing water. This is what we need to do whenever we can tell the river of life is not flowing; begin to dig into the Word and ask the Lord for a new baptism in the Holy Spirit. For Delawareans, it should be of interest that Isaac called one of his wells Rehoboth, which means 'roominess' (Verse 22).

In Exodus 17, we read about the children of Israel running out of water and demanding that Moses do something about it. In response, Moses cried out to God who said, *"Take your rod and go to the rock in Horeb* (the Mountain of God, Exodus 3:1) *and smite it and water shall come out of it."* Sometime later, the people were again out of water and demanding that Moses do something. God said to Moses, *"Gather the people together, take your rod and speak to the rock and it shall give forth water"* (Numbers 20:8) Moses apparently didn't hear God say, "Speak to the rock," so he smote it once again and the water came out. But God was angry that he didn't follow His instructions and said Moses would not lead the people into the Promised Land.

This story is very significant. It is a picture of Jesus, our Rock, being smitten (crucified and resurrected), which resulted in the outpouring of the Holy Spirit. John 7:39 says, *"The Holy Spirit was not yet given, because Jesus was not yet glorified."* The Holy Spirit then fell upon the 120 believers on the day of Pentecost. The second time Moses struck the rock was a mistake. He was told to speak to it. This is a picture of our day when we're out of water (the Holy Spirit). We're not to crucify Jesus a second time, but simply ask in faith for the gift of the Holy Spirit. (Luke 11:13) The children of Israel knew that to live they had to have water. Likewise, Christians need to realize that to live a life pleasing to the Lord they must have the Holy Spirit flowing through them.

## Acknowledge

Proverbs 3:6 says, *"In all your ways acknowledge Him and He will direct your paths."* The root of the word acknowledge means to know; therefore, to acknowledge receiving a letter is to say I know you sent me a letter. It also has the connotation of appreciation and of responding. When someone reaches out to shake your hand, you respond with your hand. With all these meanings in mind, we should read Proverbs 3:6 with more understanding and compliance.

Have you ever written to someone and didn't get a response, given someone a gift without any thanks, helped someone out of a jam, or even spoken to someone and received no response? I have, and I confess my sin in being quick to write them off as stupid, or weird, or hopeless. I really do feel like their actions are unforgivable, but of course, I know that we must forgive them. This failure must be pretty common, since almost every invitation ends with, "Please respond."

I will tell you about a couple of experiences I have had that are still vivid in my mind. I was walking home from high school one day and caught up with a classmate. I said something and got no response. I tried again and still no response. After one more time with no response, I gave up. We just walked on in silence. That was one of my longest walks. A few years later, a girl in my Sunday school class was getting married. As a wedding gift, I gave her a twenty-dollar bill, which was a big sacrifice for me. Never heard a word. I've written letters, helped people in a jam, loaned money, etc., and no response. One especially irking situation for me is when I am asked to play for a wedding and never receive a word of thanks.

Well, enough already. It happens to everyone. We must admit it leaves a bad feeling towards such people. However, here's the rub, we all do the same thing. As Paul says in Romans 2:1, we like to judge others about something that we do ourselves. One of the worst things we do is forget to thank the Lord for His goodness. Just take food, for one example. Oh, how we enjoy it, but how many bother to say thanks before or after eating. Is God offended? Jesus told the story of healing 10 lepers and only being thanked by one. I believe that He must have been offended. Non-Christians can be excused of course, since they don't trust in Christ, but what excuse does the Christian have? Paul says in Colossians 3:15, *"Be ye thankful"* and *"Whatever you do, give thanks to God"* (Verse 17). *"Continue in prayer with thanksgiving."* (Colossians 4:2) *"In everything give thanks. This is God's will."* (1 Thessalonians 5:18) It is very clear that He expects a response. We should be thankful that God stoops to teach us these things, and for all the other things He teaches us. Because of the Word He has given us, we know where we came from and where we're going. We know we've been taken out of a pit and adopted into a royal family. We live in the happiest state imaginable and have the Almighty God as our friend, and yet, are we acknowledging these blessings?

For those who forget what we should be thankful for, turn in your Bible to Psalm 103. David says, *"Bless the Lord O my Soul, and all that is within me bless His holy name and forget not all His benefits."* Then he lists many of them:

Verse 3 -forgiveness and healing;
Verse 4 -redemption, loving kindness and tender mercies;
Verse 5 -good food and renewed youth;
Verse 6 - the administration of justice and fairness for the oppressed;
Verse 7 - the revelation of His ways;
Verse 13-the fatherhood of God and the compassion He has for us.

This is just a starter list of spiritual blessings. Memorize it and then add to it day by day in your journal. In our daily routine, we should thank God for giving us a new day, a good breakfast, a job, a car, a home, a family, friends, etc., etc. What about sunshine, clouds, trees, flowers, grass, shrubs, sidewalks, paved roads, etc? What about health, energy, the ability to walk, run, play games, and go shopping? The list goes on and on for those who have eyes to see.

One of the main charges against unbelievers is that they take everything for granted. *"They see God's goodness everywhere, but they're not thankful. So, they are without excuse."* (Romans 1:20-21) *"In the last days men shall be---unthankful."* (2 Timothy 3:2) Surely, we don't want to be part of that crowd. Andrae Crouch said it so well: "The voices of a million angels could not express my gratitude. All that I am, or ever hope to be, I owe it all to Thee. To God be the glory for the things He has done." For a helpful exercise, memorize Psalm 150 and substitute the word 'thanks' for 'praise'. Let that be your last words to the Lord before you go to sleep.

## Amazing Grace

I wouldn't be surprised if a pollster announced that 'Amazing Grace' is the most misunderstood song of all time. Do people really know what they're singing? Do they mean it? I have my doubts.

Take the title. How many know what grace means? Someone suggested we use the word as an acronym, giving us this meaning: God's Riches at Christ's Expense. But how many know what that means? It takes a dedicated Christian to understand and appreciate what Jesus did for us.

To help non-Christians see, and maybe understand, what they're singing, I offer this interpretation: Grace is the love, favor and compassion of God toward undeserving sinners. It encompasses the whole of God's plan of salvation, such as Jesus dying on the cross for our sins and giving us the Holy Spirit to help us overcome sin. It is amazing grace because no one in the whole world would lay down His life for someone that hated Him, but that's what Jesus did. Some of the very people that sing Amazing Grace hate God. How do I know that? Because God is universally ignored and rejected. Try to introduce some thoughts about God in any discussion and see how quickly they tell you to get lost. These are the people that Jesus died for. Amazing!

Grace saved 'a wretch like me'. Wretch means worthless, despised, contemptible, miserable, etc. Not many people will agree they are that bad, but that's God's assessment. He says even our righteous, good deeds are like filthy rags. (Isaiah 64:6) The reason is that, until we receive Christ as our Savior, we are children of Adam, born in sin and enemies of God. Nothing we do is acceptable to God until we're born again into God's family.

'I once was lost' - I was blind. Lost and blind is about the worst possible situation to be in. Lost because we're separated from God; blind because we're not able to discern between right and wrong and see the need for a savior. 'I was found' -- I could see. Who was it that found us? Who gave us sight? Grace is another name for Jesus. It was Jesus who found us and gave us sight.

'Twas grace that taught my heart to fear and grace my fears relieved.' What was the fear? It was the fear of suddenly falling into the lake of fire. (Revelation 21:8) Only Jesus could relieve that fear. 'How precious did that grace appear, the hour I first believed.' When we're first saved, we're on fire for God. You can read about the first Christians in Acts 2 and 3.

'When we've been there 10,000 years, bright shining as the sun, we've no less days to sing God's praise, than when we first begun.' This is eternal life, given to all who turn to the Lord and ask for His salvation.

## Be Ye Perfect

A friend and I were discussing the Bible command to be perfect. He suddenly said, "You don't think you're perfect, do you?" He had me there. I thought so but didn't have a ready answer. In Matthew 5:48, Jesus says, "*Be ye therefore perfect even as your Father in heaven is perfect.*" I can hear you say, "That's impossible, so we can forget it." But there are other passages that say the same things. For example, Matthew 22:37 says, "*You shall love the Lord your God with all your heart, with all your soul, with all your strength and with all your mind and your neighbor as yourself. This is the first and greatest commandment.*" I hear you saying, "That's impossible, too. You'd have to be perfect to keep that commandment." Here's another one, Matthew 13:23 says, "*He that received seed into good ground is he that hears the Word and understands it and bears fruit; some 100-fold, some 60-fold and some 30-fold.*" One hundred-fold means 100%, and I'm pretty sure that means perfect. One more verse is Hebrews 6:1, *"Let us go on unto perfection."*

What do we do with a verse that we think is impossible? We know we can't just disregard what Jesus says. The only thing we can do is keep studying the Bible and asking the Lord for enlightenment. He does promise to reveal all truth to us (John 15:26), so it shouldn't be too long before we get to Romans 7:18 and find that Paul was struggling with the same problem. He says, *"I know that in me dwells no good thing,"* i.e., no ability to obey the commandment to love God and to be perfect. Verse 22 says, *"I delight in your commandment, but I can't obey it. O wretched man that I am. Who will free me from this weakness, failure, inability? Who will rescue me?"* Then Paul had an epiphany (revelation). *"Thank God, it has been done by Jesus Christ our Lord."* What Paul couldn't do and what we can't do, Jesus did for us.

He put his perfection in our account, so that we can say with Paul, Thank God, I am perfect through Christ.' The next chapter of Romans begins, *"There is, therefore, (because of Christ) now no condemnation to them who are in Christ Jesus, who walk after the Spirit"* i.e., we are perfect. We can stand before the judge without the least bit of fear. There are two requirements emphasized in this verse that we need to be sure of. First, that we're in Christ, and second, that we're walking (living) in the Spirit. Once He sets us free from our lost condition by our receiving Christ as Savior, we will naturally, normally, feel compelled to be a follower of Christ. We must seek and receive His Holy (pure, perfect) Spirit which will enable us to live just like He did - a perfect life, pleasing to God. (Luke 11:13) Of course, being human still, we will fall, but He will pick us up. *"If we confess our sins, He is faithful and just to forgive us our sins."* (1 John 1:9) Keep these thoughts in mind and you'll have a ready answer if anyone should ask you such a question.

A final thought, and maybe the most important. We should be asking ourselves what exactly does perfect refer to? Is it conduct, attitude, good deeds, relationships, faith, witnessing, self-control, obedience, humbleness, bravery? We get many examples from the Bible of all these qualities: the meekness of Moses (Numbers 12:3), delight in the Word of God (Psalm 1), the bravery of Gideon (Judges 6:12), the faith of Abraham (Hebrews 11:4), and many more. The one I think is most important is the love relationship. Among many examples, we'd have to say that David stands out. God said David was a man after His own heart. (Acts 13:22) You can't get a better compliment than that. And remember, David was a sinner. I'd say if you have a perfect relationship with Jesus Christ, you're perfect.

## Believing

The most important fact in the world for us to know is that a judgment day is coming. The Bible says, *"Prepare to meet thy God."* This should be done early in life, of course, but if you neglected it before, neglect it no more. We are all hanging on to life by a thread. To leave this world unprepared is a fate too horrible to contemplate.

To complete this preparation, there are some things you need to know. The first thing is that if you have never come to God before, you are on bad terms with Him. We all come from Adam. He was a notorious sinner and took us all down with him. A sinner is an enemy of God. He offends God every day mainly by just ignoring Him. The first thing you need to do is to confess this and ask for mercy. This is called repentance.

The next thing you need to know is that despite your sin God loves you and paid a huge price to be able to give you mercy. This is the Gospel, or good news. It is stated over and over in the Bible, but the most famous verse is John 3:16. As you read this verse replace the words "world" and "whosoever" with your name. This will help you make it personal. Now, tell Jesus that you do believe, and you do want everlasting life. Believe it or not, this is all you need to do to be ready for the judgment day. Remember the two thieves crucified with Jesus. One man mocked Him, the other asked Jesus to remember him. That was all it took. Jesus said, *"Today you will be with me in Paradise."* Incidentally, notice that Jesus on the center cross divides all people into two parts: believers and unbelievers.

There are many other things to consider in becoming a Christian. At least two of them are quite important. They have to do with the meaning of the word believe. As in every area of life, there is the true and there is the counterfeit. One can be sincerely convinced that a twenty-dollar bill is real, but if the judge says no, you've lost your money. In the matter of believing, there are counterfeits. One is to believe in the wrong thing. Another is to believe in the wrong way. These are subtle differences and not distinguishable to most people, but they are enough to stamp your belief a counterfeit and cause you to lose your soul.

Believing in the wrong thing probably happens gradually. A person believes in Jesus, but as he becomes involved in the work of the church, the institution becomes more and more important to him and the Savior becomes less important. Soon, without knowing it, he believes that it is the church that saves him. He forgets that the church is only a body of saved sinners. Jesus spoke about people like this in Matthew 7:22-23. They said, *"Lord, we have done this and this for you."* Jesus said, *"I never knew you."* Peter said in Acts 4:12, *"There is no other name given whereby you can be saved."*

Another misplaced belief is to think much study of the Bible brings salvation. Jesus said about these people, "You study much and think this will give you eternal life, but you never come to me." Intellectual understanding will not cut it, as they say today. Only a personal relationship with the Lord is acceptable. Another illustration from the Bible is found in Luke 20:42. Mary and Martha were preparing supper for Jesus. Martha saw Mary just sitting and listening to Jesus, so she complained, but Jesus said, "Martha, you are working hard, but there's only one thing a person needs. That's what Mary has chosen, and that's what she will keep." Mary had found the secret.

Believing the wrong way has to do with the way you respond to the gospel. True believing is a matter of the heart. It always results in a dramatic change in lifestyle. The Bible describes it as a new birth or beginning, as becoming a new creation, as receiving God's Spirit, as seeing the light, and many other explanations. If this isn't happening, then you are believing in the wrong way. For illustration, think of someone giving you a hundred dollars. You would certainly show your appreciation. If someone gave you a million dollars, you would be ecstatic. You'd run to them and exclaim repeatedly how they blessed you and changed your life. Now think of sitting on death row waiting to be executed. The person you injured appears and offers to take your punishment. We're all in this situation. If this unthinkable offer doesn't grab you, then you just don't get it. A famous poet wrote that you could damn a person with faint praise. That's what you're doing when you say you know that Jesus died for you, but your only response is to attend church once in a while and pay some dues. Jesus talks about people being lukewarm and how they will be cast out. He talks about people that worship with their lips, but not with their heart.

I remember the first time I really understood the Gospel. I knew my life was not my own anymore. I had to live for Him who died for me. A very enlightening scripture on this is 1 Peter 2:2. Peter says that just as a baby is born with a built-in desire for milk, so everybody born into God's family has a built-in desire to know God by reading His Word. If you have no desire, then you do not believe correctly. The thing to do is start all over again seeking God. Start with the Gospel of John. When you come to John 1:12, say, "Lord, I receive you." When you come to John 3:3, say, "Lord, I want to be born again." If you keep on reading and responding like this, you are believing in the right One and in the right way and will smile on Judgment Day because the Judge you will be facing is the very One you are talking to everyday.

May we all be found faithful on that great day of the Lord.

# Born Again

In a day of multiple interviews on wide ranging subjects, from global warming to global wars, little notice is given to the most important interview of all, the one between Jesus and Nicodemus about 2,000 years ago. One statement Jesus made has reverberated down through the centuries, but it's still little understood. The statement 'you must be born again' is found in John 3:3. Jesus used such a statement, no doubt, to raise some questions in Nicodemus' mind. What did Jesus mean? How is it possible to be born a second time? Where did such a strange idea come from? It certainly sounds weird to think you can be born again.

Nicodemus was non-plussed. He was a member of the strictest sect of the Jews and was supposed to be very knowledgeable. He had seen Jesus do some miracles and he knew that the Pharisees had rejected him. Being curious, he decided to see for himself, (Oh, that more people would do that!) so he visited Jesus. He said, "Rabbi, you must come from God since no one can do the miracles you do." Then Jesus made His statement, "*You must be born again.*" It would seem like Jesus was a little short with him. He made no acknowledgement of the compliment, no small talk. I think Jesus just couldn't wait to tell him the most important truth of all time. Jesus went right to the point; you've got to be born again. It should have taken Nicodemus back to the Book of Genesis, which he was supposed to know by heart, then he could have said to Jesus, or at least to himself, "Yes, yes, I see that. Our first birth was into Adam's family who rebelled against God and was cast out of Eden. Yes, of course, we all come from Adam, so it would take a second birth to get back into God's family. It's God giving humans a second chance." But Nicodemus, a ruler of the Jews, hadn't done his homework. He was just as befuddled as plenty of people are today. He asked, "How can a man be born when he is old?" Jesus then explained about being born of God's Spirit. Nicodemus, still befuddled, asked, "How can this be?" Then Jesus let him have it. "*Are you a ruler of the Jews and don't know these things?*" What a dereliction of duty and what an outrage for Nicodemus, an esteemed ruler and teacher, to be ignorant of the most important thing he and his people were supposed to know. It was inexcusable. The Good News; however, is that Nicodemus paid attention to Jesus and was born again.

The world today is mostly in the same situation as Nicodemus, trusting in their leaders to get them into heaven. Not too many take the initiative like he did to find out the truth. The Jewish leaders misled the people all through the Bible and capped it off by killing their Messiah and causing them to be scattered all over the world. They've been paying for their mistake for 2,000 years. If you're a church member and have never been born again, you're still in Satan's family. If you see how precarious your situation is, and repent of your sins, and ask Jesus to be your savior, you will be born again in an instant. The thief on the cross was saved by calling Jesus Lord and asking him to remember him. Jesus said, "*Today you will be with me in Paradise.*" (Luke 23:42-43) The thief didn't have any time to grow spiritually, but you probably do. The key verse on growing and knowing you've been born again is 1 Peter 2:2, "*As a newborn baby you will desire the milk of the Word*" (the Bible). The Living Bible reads, "*You will cry for it as a baby cries for milk.*"

Once you start studying the Word, you soon find out that this new life is totally different from your old life. For example, you will read, "Love your enemy." Your old life would laugh and say, "You must be crazy." As just one more example, Jesus said, "*The Son (Jesus) can do nothing by himself. He does only what he sees the Father do. For whatever things God does, these doeth the Son.*" (John 5:19) This one verse should tell you you're in a different world. Your purpose now is to become a little Christ, or Christian, under God's control, just as Jesus was. The disciples spent three years with him and still, at his crucifixion, they all ran away. You can see, it is not an easy road, but God can make it happen. "*If you continue in my Word, then are you my disciples indeed and you shall know the truth and the truth shall make you free.*" (John 8:31)

# Broken

Matthew 21:44 says, *"..whosoever shall fall on this stone shall be broken, but on whomsoever it shall fall, it will grind him to powder."* In this verse, God gives us a dramatic contrast between the saved and the lost. You either fall on Him and are broken, or He falls on you and you will be smashed. Not a pleasant picture, but it is the only way out of a horrendous situation. To fall on Him is to realize that you nailed Jesus to the cross, that you are a sinner in the hands of an angry God, and that you are hanging over the flames of hell by a thread. When you see this, you will be broken into pieces. David was broken and described his experience in Psalm 51. Verse 8 says, *"You have crushed me and broken me."* (Modern English). This is the only way out of our sinful condition. Psalm 34:18 says, *"The Lord is close to the brokenhearted, and saves those who are of a contrite spirit."* Psalm 51 is the perfect example of brokenness. It is hard to imagine how David could sin like he did and not be bothered by it for so long. But, when the Lord finally got through to him, he was truly broken. We, like David, need a special revelation of how hideous sin is.

The tragedy on September 11, 2001 was probably the worst crime ever committed on American soil and has caused us to take a hard look at the people that could do such a terrible thing. Our hearts go out to the victims and their families at the sorrow they experienced but think for a moment. We all belong to a fallen race. We all are guilty of terrible sin. Jesus was despised and rejected, not by someone else, but by us. He was wounded and bruised. He was oppressed and afflicted. He was cut off out of the land of the living. We cut Him out of our lives. If we read these phrases in Isaiah 53 without seeing that we were the ones who nailed Jesus to the cross, we have missed something. But, if they cause us to identify with David in his sorrow and brokenness for sin, then we will receive God's mercy. David said by inspiration, *"The sacrifices that God accepts are a broken spirit; a broken and a contrite heart O God, you will not despise."* (Psalm 51)

In 1 Chronicles 4:10, (the prayer of Jabez), it says, *"And Jabez called on the God of Israel, saying, Oh, that you would bless me indeed and enlarge my coast, and that your hand might be with me, and that you would keep me from evil, that it may not grieve me! And God granted him that which he requested."* This prayer seems to be quite ordinary, yet it caused the Lord to stop what He was doing and call attention to it. As you read the prayer, you can sense right away why God took notice of it. It begins with Oh! This is an interjection which expresses strong passion, which means suffering, which indicates brokenness. This was not a "lay me down to sleep" prayer. Jabez was a broken man. We don't know what caused him to cry out. It had to be something like the man in Psalm 34:4, *"I sought the Lord and He delivered me."* Verse 6 says, *"This poor man cried to the Lord and the Lord saved him out of all his trouble."* Verse 15 says, *"The eyes of the Lord are upon the righteous and His ears are open to their cry."*

Peter was crushed when he realized what he had done. He cursed and swore saying, *"I know not the man."* (Matthew 26:74) Jesus turned and looked at him. Then Peter remembered that Jesus had said, *"You will deny me three times."* Peter went out and wept bitterly. (Luke 22:60-62) He was broken a little more when Jesus asked him three times if he really loved Him. (John 21:15-17) Jesus came to bind up the broken hearted. (Luke 4:18) The way He did this was to be broken for us. 1 Corinthians 11:24 says, *"This is my body broken for you."* For those who refuse to be broken and accept God's salvation, there is no other remedy. Remember Adam, Cain, King Saul, Judas, the other thief on the cross, and many others that paid dearly for their stubbornness.

Isaiah 51:1 says, *"Look to the rock from whence you are hewn."* (Isaiah 51:1) *"A stone,* (a peculiar people, godly people) *cut out of the mountain* (ungodly people) *without* (human) *hands shall be established and shall stand forever."* (Daniel 2:44) *"The stone became a great mountain* (nation) *and filled the whole earth."* (Daniel 2:35) *"And the temple was built of stone made ready before it was brought to the site, so that there was neither hammer, nor ax, nor any tool of iron heard while it was in building."* (1 Kings 6:7) *"Is not My Word like a hammer that breaks the rock in pieces?"* (Jeremiah 23:27) *"You also, as living stones, are built up a spiritual house."* (1Peter 2:5)

These verses are telling us that Christians are being taken out of the world (ungodly) not by hands of people, but by God (John 1:13), and will become the Kingdom of God during the millennium. The important part for us to see is that the stones are made ready before they become part of the building. In other words, you get broken before He comes.

There will be no getting broken after. Then it will be too late. *"Now is the accepted time. Now is the day of salvation."* (2 Corinthians 6:2)

## Catastrophes?

Many people are asking why, if there is a god, does he allow such terrible things to happen such as the Tsunami, and the destruction of the World Trade Center. They say, "If there is a god, he must be too weak to do anything about calamities, or he doesn't care." Their diagnosis is wrong on both counts. God is Almighty, and He does care, but He is also just. He doesn't arbitrarily take something that doesn't belong to Him. If He did, He would be a thief.

Most people think this world belongs to God. There is even a hymn that churches sing with gusto, "This is my Father's world. Let me never forget, that though the wrong seems oft so strong, God is the ruler yet." If we go by the Bible, we have to say these words are wrong. Of course, God created the world, but He gave it to Adam and Eve, and they forfeited it to Satan. God said to them, *"Subdue the earth and have dominion over every living thing."* (Genesis 1:28) But, Adam and Eve disobeyed God and lost their lordship of the earth. It passed to Satan. We see this in Luke 4:6, where Satan is tempting Jesus. He says, *"All this power* (of the world) *will I give you and the glory of them, for that is delivered unto me, and to whomsoever I will, I give it. If you will worship me, all will be yours."* Satan owns the world. What kind of proprietor is Satan? Jesus said, *"He is a murderer - he is a liar."* (John 8:44) *"He comes to steal, kill and destroy."* (John 10:10) *"The world is in Satan's lap, under his power and control."* (1 John 5:19)

Satan hates us with a passion, and as Jesus said, he wants to steal, kill, and destroy us. Since most people reject God and pledge allegiance to Satan, they belong to him and he can do as he pleases with them, up to a point. There is such a thing as common grace, where God is good to all, good and bad. He sends the rain on the just and unjust. Satan can only go as far as God allows him. On the other hand, there are laws like the law of gravity. If you break them, you can expect a catastrophe. Proverbs 2:1 says, *"He that being oft reproved hardens his neck, shall suddenly be destroyed and that without remedy."* The flood that destroyed the world was the result of the total wickedness of the people. Sodom and Gomorrah were also destroyed for the same reason. Many terrible things happen as the result of wrong choices.

Deuteronomy 30:1 says, *"I have set before you life and good, death and evil - therefore, choose life."* Avoid calamities. There are also the trials and tribulations that God allows to test us. 1 Peter 4:12 says, *"Think it not strange concerning the fiery trial which is to try you - but rejoice as you are partakers of Christ's sufferings."* The great Apostle Paul said the Lord gave him a thorn in the flesh to keep him humble. He prayed that the Lord would remove it, but God said, *"My grace is sufficient for you."*

Through the centuries, catastrophes have almost been the norm. In Revelation 6:9, we read about people that were murdered just because they believed in God, *"Slain for the Word of God and for the testimony they held."* This is the ultimate catastrophe and it's happening even as I write this. The best we can do is take comfort from the scripture, *"The Son of God was manifested that He might destroy the works of the devil."* (1 John 3:8) Let's pray that it happens soon.

# Choices

Every day we make hundreds of choices. Some of them seem to have no consequence but mixed up in the middle of all those easy choices are the ones that are critical, ones that have eternal consequences. You choose where to sit when you come into a room. Most likely, it would be of no consequence, but the possibility is that it could have eternal consequences. You could say a word to your neighbor that would change his life and his family's life for generations.

I have made choices in my life that have completely turned my life around, but at the time, I didn't have any idea that they were critical.

Some of them were good, some bad. I've learned it pays to pray about everything. No doubt, that's why Paul said, *"Pray without ceasing."*

Listed below are some crucial choices made by well-known people in the Bible and the consequences thereof:

## Genesis 2:17, 3:14-29

God told Adam and Eve to stay away from a certain tree. They could eat of every other tree, just stay away from one. They were told that the consequences of disobedience would be death. This should have been a great help in making the right choice, but they failed anyway. That consequence brought the curse of death on the human race.

## Genesis 4

God commanded Cain and Abel both to bring a blood sacrifice for the covering of their sins. Abel brought a lamb (right choice).

Cain brought a basket of fruit (wrong choice). God loved Cain so much that he even reasoned with him and told him that he could change his mind (vs. 7). However, Cain got angry and made another bad choice. He killed his brother. This brought a curse on him and his family. Right after that, he made another bad choice. *"He was out from the presence of God."* (Gen. 4:1) He could have chosen to repent, and God would have forgiven him.

## Genesis 6

God promised Abraham a son, but when God delayed the fulfillment, Abraham chose to take matters into his own hands. He had the child, Ishmael, with his Egyptian maid. Ishmael's descendants, the Arabs, have been at war with Israel ever since. It was a bad choice.

## Genesis 22:7-9

Isaac was faced with a hard decision. He was probably a young adult when he was climbing a mountain to make a sacrifice unto the Lord with his father. In verse 7, Isaac asks, *"Where is the lamb?"* When Isaac heard he was to be that sacrifice, he had a choice to make; to run or submit! He submitted. Because of that choice, he became a type of Christ, submitting to the cross. In our walk with the Lord, we often have to make choices about either running from or submitting to God's dealings.

## Genesis 25:31-34

Esau was the firstborn and was to inherit all the blessings. However, one day he became very hungry and sold his birthright to Jacob for something to eat. How many people give up their inheritance in Christ for a little material pleasure? He did not value God's covenant promises. Esau made a bad choice and all his descendants suffered for it. So many times, our choices affect many others around us!

## Hebrews 11:25

Moses was the opposite of Esau. He chose to suffer affliction with the people of God, rather than enjoy the pleasures of sin for a short while. Because of that good choice, Moses became the greatest leader this world has ever known.

## Nation of Israel

Before Israel was to enter the Promise land, Moses gave them this warning: *"I have set before you life and death, blessing and cursing; therefore choose life, that both you and your seed may live."* (Deut. 30:19)

## Joshua 24:15

Joshua, the successor of Moses, also warned the people to stay with God. He told them, *"Choose you this day whom you will serve...as for me and my house, we will serve the Lord."* But Israel made so many wrong choices that God let them be conquered and scattered all over the world.

## 1 Samuel 10:8, 13:8 and 31:2

King Saul was given strict orders by Samuel twice, and chose to disobey both times. For this, he lost the kingdom and his life.

## 1 Samuel 23:17

Jonathan made a sad choice. He was the Crown Prince of Israel, but God revealed to him that David was to be the next king. Jonathan loved David dearly and was glad to take the lower position. So, he pledged his allegiance to David, but when he met David in the wilderness, he wasn't willing to stay with him. He would return to his father, King Saul. Then a war broke out and Saul and all his sons were killed. If Jonathan had stayed with David, he would, doubtless, have lived to rule with David. (Incidentally, Christians who aren't willing to go all out for Jesus will miss the golden opportunity of ruling with Christ in the millennium.)

## Psalm 27:4

David, one of the greatest men that ever lived, made good choices. In one sentence, he gives the key to success: "*One thing have I desired* (or chosen) *of the Lord, that will I seek after, that I may dwell in the house of the Lord all the days of my life, to behold the beauty of the Lord and to inquire in his temple.*" David was a man after God's own heart! We won't go into the one big mistake he made at this time.

## 1 Samuel 2:33

Eli chose not to discipline his two sons and instead of living the good life, they died in their youth.

## Judges 19

Samson was chosen by the Lord to be a judge of Israel. He would have made a wonderful leader, but he had a weakness for women, and he chose to give in to it rather than fight it. He paid with his life.

## Ruth 1:16

Ruth and Orpah were two Moabite women who married the two sons of Naomi, an Israelite. They both learned of the salvation of the Lord. When Naomi decided to move back to Israel, they had to choose to go or stay. Ruth chose to go with Naomi. She said, *"Your God will be my God."* She was rewarded with the honor of being David's great grandmother. Orpah was never heard of again.

## Esther 4:13

Esther was the Queen, but she could only see the King when he invited her. Anyone entering his court without an invitation would be put to death. When a law was passed to kill all the Jews in the land, Esther had to choose risking her life to see the King to ask for help, or to ignore the situation. She chose the first and saved thousands of lives.

At the crucifixion of our Lord we see two thieves were crucified with him; one chose to scoff at him, one chose to believe Him. One went to hell, the other to heaven.

Two disciples betrayed the Lord. One chose to repent and receive God's mercy (Peter), the other chose to kill himself (Judas). One went to heaven, the other went to hell. Choices that face us every day:

To walk the broad or the narrow way. (Matthew 7:13)

To build on sand or on the Rock. (Matthew 7:24)

To build with gold and silver, or wood and hay. (1 Corinthians 3:12)

To walk in the Spirit or in the flesh. (Romans 8:1, 14)

To open the door to Jesus or not. [Revelations 3:20 (not salvation)]

To let the Word of God dwell in you (memorize) or not. (Colossians 3:16)

To be filled with the Spirit or not. (Ephesians 5:18)

To be witnesses unto Jesus or not. (Acts 1:8)

To keep yourself unspotted from the world or not. (James 1:27)

The Lord has blessed us with free will, but He lets us know there are consequences. Deuteronomy 38:30 describes the blessings and curses that go with choices and ends with, "*I have set before you life and death. Therefore, choose life.*" (Deuteronomy 30:19)

# Church History

The history of the church began hundreds of years before its actual birthday. It began with the prophecy of Joel 2:28 and Zechariah 12:10. The Lord says, "*It shall come to pass that I will pour out my Spirit on all flesh and your sons and your daughters will prophesy. – I will pour out my Spirit upon the servants and handmaids.*" Hundreds of years later, another prophet appeared named John the Baptist, and announced that the promise of God was about to be fulfilled. He pointed to Jesus and said, "*I baptize you in water, but He will baptize you in the Holy Spirit.*"(Matthew 3:11) This is saying, "I give you the gift of repentance, but He will give you the gift of power."

Soon after Jesus began His ministry, He was speaking to the woman at the well and said, "*The water I will give you will be like a well springing up unto eternal life.*" (John 4) He spoke of the Holy Spirit. Sometime later, at the great Feast of Tabernacles, Jesus cried out saying, "*Whoever believes in me, out of his innermost being shall flow rivers of living water. This spake He of the Holy Spirit.*" (John 7:33) Toward the end of His ministry, He reminded the disciples that the promised Holy Spirit would soon be given to them, and they would be endued with power from on high. (Luke 24:47) After the resurrection, He told them not to go away, but to wait in Jerusalem for the baptism in the Spirit. (Acts 1:5) Ten days later, on the day of Pentecost, 120 people had gathered together in the Upper Room, all in one accord, worshipping the Lord, and the promise was fulfilled. The Holy Spirit came upon each one. It was described as a mighty rushing wind that filled the room. They all began praising God in different tongues (or languages). Crowds came to see what was happening, and Peter rose up to explain what it was all about. The first thing he said, was that the coming of the Holy Spirit upon them was what Joel had predicted long ago. He ended his sermon with these words, *"This promised gift is to you and to your children and to all that are far off."* (Acts 2:41) Three thousand souls were saved at that meeting! The next day, Peter was preaching again to a large crowd and five thousand were saved. Later, at a prayer meeting, the whole building shook. (Acts 4:31) This was the kind of power Jesus was talking about in Luke 24:47. The Jewish leaders were furious about all this and threatened to kill Peter and John, but they didn't dare, because so many people were now converts. This was the beginning of the church. It was such a powerful move of God that onlookers said, "These people have turned the world upside down."

These kinds of events should be considered the normal church life. I can hear you saying, "What happened? What church is like that today?" Well, there had to be a colossal failure on the part of the new converts to grow spiritually. Paul says in 1 Corinthians 3, *"You are still spiritual babies."* They also failed to walk in the Spirit. Paul says in Galatians 3:1, *"O foolish Galatians, you can't go back to living in the flesh after being filled with the Spirit."* Then of course, there were plenty of false leaders. Peter said, *"There will be false prophets among you who will make merchandise of you, doing anything to get your money."* (2 Peter 26:1-3)

It's hard to believe that the people would backslide after such a tremendous beginning, but that's what they did. The false leaders pulled the wool over their eyes and took over the business. How did they do it? First, they used the old stratagem, divide and conquer. They split the people into two classes, the ordinary, common people, sometimes called the laity, and the elite, or clergymen. This pretty much killed the church. Most people are lazy, and when a few say they'll take care of everything, the many say, "Wonderful, we can take it easy now." Up till then, the meetings were characterized by sharing, as described in 1 Corinthians 14:26, *"Everyone has a psalm, a doctrine, a tongue, an interpretation, a revelation."* Paul had urged them to covet (desire) earnestly, the best gifts, especially prophecy. (1 Corinthians 12:31, 14:39) For a while, Paul was proud of them. He said in 1 Corinthians 1:5, *"You come behind in no gift. You've been enriched in all utterance and in all knowledge."* That was the high noon of the church. But, with the false leaders taking over, all of this ended. The wonderful promise of people being filled with the Holy Spirit came to a screeching halt. The clergy said they would take care of everything. From then on, it was what some call easy, or cheap; grace came to mean becoming a member, paying your dues, and showing up once in a while. The gospel message was watered down, water baptism became water sprinkle, join a confirmation class and you're in for sure. If someone asks, "What happened to the Holy Spirit baptism?" The answer became, "Oh, that happens when you join the church."

Well, as anyone could foresee, the church went into a steep decline. All of this was foreknown and foretold in Revelation 2 and 3, where Jesus describes the church age. From these two chapters, it looks like the church was a failed endeavor, but if we look carefully, we will see that in every letter to these churches, Jesus ends with a challenge to individuals, *"He that overcomes* (or conquers) *shall be rewarded."* It seems clear that the Lord is not expecting an overcoming church but overcoming individuals.

It was a long time after the first century that God again began to move. The reformation in 1500 was a true move of God setting the stage for the Holy Spirit revival by restoring the cardinal doctrines of justification by faith and priesthood of all believers. It wasn't until 1900 that the church experienced a true revival. Some people started reading the Bible and saw that they were missing something. They began seeking the Lord and He graciously restored to them the promised Holy Spirit. From then till today, the Holy Spirit has been moving all over the world. Some see this as a fulfillment of Luke 14:16-24, where the people that were first invited to the supper refused to come, so the Lord said go out and invite everyone, the poor, the lame, whoever wants to come. The marriage supper of the Lamb is about to take place. Everyone is invited, but as always, most people are too busy to heed the call. They will miss the greatest event of all history. For those who want to be there, this is the promise. *"If you, being evil, give good gifts to your children, how much more will your heavenly Father give the Holy Spirit to them that ask Him."* (Luke 11:13)

## Close Calls

A pit is a deep hole in the ground, used as a trap to capture someone or imprison them. We've all been caught in traps or pits of one sort or another, and the Lord says we should remember how He delivered us. The Lord says, *"Look to the pit from whence ye are dug."* (Isaiah 51:1) David said, *"The Lord brought me out of a horrible pit."* (Psalm 40:2) Of course, we were all born in a pit. David said, *"I was born in sin."* (Psalm 51:5) We should constantly remember and thank the Lord for pulling us out of that one. But it is also important and healthy to remember the pits and the close calls that we've experienced in our daily lives. Close calls are a little different from pits, but both are life threatening, near death experiences. *"The devil goes about as a roaring lion seeking whom he may devour."* (1 Peter 5:8) I'm sure if it weren't for guardian angels, I'd have been devoured many years ago.

Our close calls certainly don't compare with the Bible heroes like Jacob facing 400 men (Genesis 32:6), Joseph being thrown into a pit (Genesis 37:20), Daniel thrown into the lion's den (Daniel 6:16), the three Hebrews thrown into the furnace (Daniel 3:23), or Paul being stoned to near death (Acts 14:19). But the one thing they all had in common was facing a horrible death, which is pretty much what I faced more than once and knowing that God cared enough to intervene on my behalf certainly is something to think about. I'd like to tell you about several of them, so bear with me. That's like a preacher saying, "I have so much material, I don't know where to start." A little boy said, "Please start near the end!"

Actually, I'll just pick out a couple like the time a shark nearly got me.

My first close call was falling off a fishing pier when I was four or five years old. The relatives talked about that for a long time.

My second was too long to describe here, but the sharp corner of a spade just missed my eye, not life threatening, but a horrible disaster for a young kid.

My friend and I took a canoe out in the ocean. It was calm as a lake, but we turned over. We were at least a mile out. It was late afternoon and no boats were in sight. It had begun to look hopeless when we spotted a coast guard blimp. But how could they see two heads bobbing in the ocean? Believe it or not, they came right to us, a huge massive ship, right on top of us. They let down a rope ladder and said, "Climb up." I couldn't believe our good fortune, but my friend said, "Wait, I can't leave my canoe." The captain said, "We'll see if we can find a fishing boat." You can believe I was disappointed. In a little while a boat came along and turned the canoe over. I was only about 16, so I never realized how close we came to drowning. I didn't know the Lord then, so I thought it was good luck that saved us.

I was on a freighter going to Europe, when a nor'easter, the worst kind of storm, came up. In the middle of the night, the lifeboat alarm went off. We all rushed up to the deck and got the lifeboats ready. We stood there waiting for the command to lower them. The ship was pitching like a wild horse. All of us knew we'd never make it. We waited until dawn, when the captain announced that there had been a short circuit that caused the boat alarm to go off. You would have to have been there to know how we felt. We could so easily have been lying at the bottom of the ocean, or worse yet, been in some fish's gullet.

Probably my closest call was World War II. The day after Pearl Harbor, my college roommate and I drove to Philadelphia to enlist in the Air Force. We knew that two years of college were required, which we had, so we were as good as in. To our amazement, they checked things out and said our college wasn't accredited, so they couldn't accept us. It was unbelievable. Looking back, I realize that practically everyone I knew who enlisted right away lost their lives.

We were staying at Hilton Head Island, where a couple of us were swimming. The tide was low, so we had to go pretty far out. The shrimp boats were close by. I started swimming toward the beach when a shark grabbed my foot. I kicked and screamed, and it let go. I pulled out all the stops in getting to shore. It took 36 stitches to close all the wounds. I think the shark let go to get something better than a foot. Every time I think of this one, I weep, thinking of God's mercy and my failure to give Him thanks. For some strange reason, I never thought of it. The doctors patching me up said the shrimp boats were the cause of sharks being there.

I was in a sailboat far out on the Chesapeake Bay when the sky became as dark as night and the wind began to blow like a hurricane. The boat turned over. I was young and strong, so I was able to right it, but every time I tried to get in, it turned over again. After many times, I just wanted to rest, which meant resting at the bottom of the bay. I just barely heard the power motorboat, which rescued me.

While I was in London, I crossed a busy street; looking, as usual, to the left, when a speeding car missed me by a hair. I had looked the wrong way.

I was a passenger in a car towing a loaded trailer. Everybody was asleep but the driver. Then he fell asleep and we began to fishtail. Luckily (providentially), there was a wide median where we had a rude awakening, shook up, but unhurt.

I stopped at a red light at a busy intersection, when a truck piled into me, pushing me right into oncoming traffic. If Satan had timed it right, I would have been hit a second time and it could have been curtains (a 1930 expression).

In the next close call, I was tugging on a sofa when something let go and I went hurtling backwards toward a sliding glass door. I smashed it with my head, sending a mass of glass shards everywhere, but I didn't go through it. I was dazed and thought for sure I was dying, but the Lord spared me again.

I parked near the corner of a one-way street, opened the door and started to get out, when a car, turning into the street, slammed into the door. One or two seconds and I would have been out of the car, right in his path.

I was starting up from a parked position and put my foot on the brake pedal. It slipped off and hit the gas pedal. If a car had been coming, it would have been a sure accident.

At a summer camp in the mountains, I had to run errands with a friend. He drove in the middle of the road, even over hills where we couldn't see oncoming cars. I held my breath many times that summer.

I was laying bricks, standing on a scaffold about 20 feet high. The laborer kept bringing up bricks, but no one was paying attention until we heard a cracking sound. We jumped on the wall, just in time.

I was laying bricks when a fight broke out. Bricks were flying. I got out of there in a hurry.

We were swimming under a bridge over Shark River. We didn't know anything about how swift the current was right there when the tide was running out, until someone warned us.

We were on a sea scout cruise. Late in the day, a storm came up. We raced for the inlet, but the storm broke just as we reached it. The skipper knew he couldn't take a chance going through the channel with rocks on both sides, so he called the Coast Guard. They came with a powerful cruiser and took us all off and through the inlet. The skipper then tried it but crashed on the rocks.

I was on a ferry crossing the English Channel, which is known for rough waters. A storm came up. Everyone thought we would turn over. We finally made it, but the headlines in the paper were all about the many boats that had capsized.

I was working in a machine shop on some big press. My hand got caught on the material and for a minute, I knew it was gone. Miraculously, I got it loose.

I thank God for pulling me out of pits and close calls. I'm glad I'm still alive. But, at my advanced age, I know that only means it's postponed and besides, death is nothing compared to escaping spiritual death. The Lord really worked a miracle in pulling me off the road to hell and putting me on the road to glory. As a teen, I loved music and played clarinet, string bass, and piano. I spent my summer evenings close to a ballroom stage, listening to famous bands. It was my dream to be in one of them. I began playing the bass in combos after high school. I was asked to play in a big band of 16 members. We played at the Sea Girt Inn, a popular dance hall. I made more in one night than on my regular job in a week. Celebrities like Jack Dempsey and Phil Harris showed up. I never had so much fun. I thought I was in heaven. I saw my dream was coming true. How could I be so lucky? Then a strange thing happened. My mother saw an article in the paper about a college opening nearby. I was interested, so we went to see about it. To make a long story short, I was soon a student in a Christian

College. They had the best preachers I had ever heard. I became a Christian and forgot all about my other dream, sold my bass, and began a brand-new lifestyle. Knowing the kind of life entertainers are exposed to and indulge in, I know that by the mercy of God, that college opened its doors and enabled me to pass from death to life. (John 5:24)

## Clues from the Story of the Birth of Christ

A clue is something that will help solve a problem of a doubtful or intricate nature. In Bible days, they were called parables, or stories that illustrated spiritual truths. No doubt, the most famous is about the prodigal son. Briefly, the son leaves home and becomes a wicked sinner. In time, he becomes desperate and returns home. The father is overjoyed to see him. The truth illustrated is that mankind, long ago, departed from God to make it on his own. Through the centuries, his situation has only gotten worse, until today, it is desperate. God wants man to know that if he will return, he will be received with joy and restored to his former happy condition. This is a glorious truth, revealed through a parable.

The birth of Christ is not a story told specifically to illustrate truth. Rather, it is an account of actual events, but its many details illustrate the truths that God wants us to know. We call these details, clues.

1. Probably the best-known clue is the very strange fact that Jesus was born in a stable with the animals. In the Bible, sinners are compared to animals. As such, they cannot enter heaven. (Rev. 22:15) So, Jesus being born among animals, in their very habitat, is a clue. It can only mean one thing. No matter how wretched, filthy, etc., we are (or think we are sometimes), He loves us and is willing to be born in us. He tells us in John 1:12, *"As many as receive Him, they have the right to become sons of God."*

2. "There was no room in the inn." This is a graphic picture of our world having no time for God. It didn't have room for Him 2,000 years ago, and it still doesn't have room today, in spite of all our time saving inventions. The room we're talking about is quality time in His presence. An hour a week is not making room. Actually, He wants to dwell in us, which suggests full time. *"We will come and make our abode with you."* (John 14:23). Jerusalem was full of religious people and yet, the innkeeper didn't know one family that he could call on in such a desperate situation. Was no one there in touch with God? If we had been living there, would somebody have said, "Oh, take them to the Smith's house?" Another thought, if Joseph had money to spare, would the innkeeper have found room for him? These are clues to the desperate condition of our world, then and now. Making room for Him is no doubt our biggest challenge, but His command is still, *"Enter your closet and shut the door and pray."* (Matthew 6:6)

3. Jesus was laid in a manger where animals feed. Think of putting your newborn baby in the dog's bowl. What condescension; more than we can ever know. What does it mean? For one thing, it suggests Jesus is food. He said, *"Except you eat me, you have no life."* (John 6:53) This was too much for some of His followers, but His command is still there.

4. Jesus was born as a helpless baby into a world where both the political system and the religious systems considered murder to be a normal part of their activities. King Herod thought nothing of killing scores of babies on the chance he'd get the newborn king. We should not be surprised to read in our daily paper of the killing going on in Africa, Indonesia and other parts of the world. Our adversary, the devil, is still out to steal, kill, and destroy all that is of God.

5. Mary submitted to being put in a terrifying situation. It was not just being poor and having to take a long hard journey, and seeming to be all alone in the world, but she knew she would be the subject of malicious gossip about her child. But, Mary was a chosen vessel. Read Mary's thoughts and words in Luke 1:46-55, and you'll see why God chose her. This passage is called "The Magnificat," a beautiful

expression of her love for God. She had to be saturated with the Word of God to be able to say something so beautiful, and this is your clue - get in the Word. Another clue, how would you respond to God if He asked you to visit the mental institution, the prisons, the flophouses, or the slums? God knew Mary would yield to Him, so she was chosen. Keep in mind that "many are called, but few are chosen." The 'many' choose not to respond.

6. Jesus was born in Bethlehem Ephrata (the house of bread, fruitful). This is an obvious clue. The Word of God is our daily bread. To be born of God and to grow, we have to read it. This could be seen as a test for you. Both house of bread and fruitful are joined together. If you're living in the house of bread, you will be fruitful. If you have no fruit, you're probably not in the Word. Jesus said, *"Man lives by every word of God."* (Matthew 4:4) He also said we should abide in the vine and bear fruit. If there's no fruit, the branch will be cut off. (John 15.)

7. Jesus, as God's son, should have been born in a palace. Mary tells us why it couldn't be (Luke 1:51-53). *"He has scattered the proud, put down the mighty, and sent the rich empty away."* God only has contempt for "big shots" that live in palaces. *"The meek shall inherit the earth."* (Psalms 37:11) Psalms 34 says, *"God is near them that are of a broken heart and saves such as be of a contrite spirit."*

8. The angel of the Lord announced the birth of Jesus to shepherds. They were the lowest of the low in that day. Why were they told instead of the priests and Pharisees? The same reason as in #7. God cannot tolerate pride and the religious system was saturated with it. Luke 2:20 gives an indication as to why the shepherds were chosen. They returned to their work praising and glorifying God. It's hard to imagine the Pharisees and Sadducees being described in this way. How do you react to some great blessing from God?

9. The angel of the Lord also announced the birth of Jesus to wise men from the East. They were Gentiles from a far country, considered by the Jews (and by God) to be dogs. So, here, right at the beginning, God

gives a big clue that Jesus was not only to be the savior of Jews, but of the whole world. This should have caused the Jews to see that Gentiles could be saved, but they missed it. Are we missing it too? Jesus said, *"He came, not to save the righteous, but sinners."* (Matthew 9:13) We should also know from the wise men, that God guides true seekers. *"If we seek Him, He <u>will</u> be found of us."* (1 Chronicles 28:9) *"You shall find me when you seek me with all your heart."* (Jeremiah 29:13) The wise men went to extraordinary lengths to find the King. *"God rewards them that diligently seek Him."* (Hebrews 11:6)

10.  The wise men brought gifts: gold, frankincense and myrrh. This is a clue that God welcomes and appreciates our gifts. We read in John 4:23 that God seeks worship. Gold stands for holiness, frankincense stands for prayers, and myrrh stands for suffering. These gifts are clues to the kind of gifts God is interested in.

11.  The most important clue of all is that Mary was to give birth to the Son of God. What happened to her is what God desires for all of us. As the seed of the Holy Spirit was planted in her, so the seed of the Holy Spirit should be planted in us. Matthew 13:18 and the following explain this process. The seed (The Word of God) is planted in good soil (a receptive heart). It will grow and develop until the Son of God is formed in us, and in the fullness of time, be revealed to the world. Paul says in Galatians 4:19, *"I travail in birth until Christ be formed in you."* Revelation 21:7 says, *"He that overcomes - shall be my son."* In Genesis 16, there is the story of Abraham's son, Isaac, being born supernaturally. The conceiving and birthing of Christ in us is like Isaac's birth, a supernatural event. Jesus was born in due time and revealed to the world. Likewise, in due time the sons of God will be revealed to the world. We read in Romans 8:19 that the whole world is waiting for the manifestation of the sons of God. Romans 8:29 says that Jesus is the firstborn of many brothers. Colossians 1:27 says, *"Christ in you is the hope of glory."*

We believe this event will soon take place. Woe to the people that miss this, this most glorious event of all time. A trillion dollars couldn't buy this privilege; and yet, it is free for the asking.

## Creation or Big Bang

Murphy's Law: If anything can go wrong, it will! If everything happened by chance, like a big bang, where was Murphy's Law, and how did everything go right for us? A million things could have gone wrong. The law of probability would say the odds of everything going right would be trillions to one. For example, the air we breathe is just the right mix. How did that happen? The same with the water, sunlight, soil, gravity, night and day, trees, animals, plants, insects and the big systems like the oceans and water cycle, the food chain, rainforests, and that's just considering the natural world.

With the slightest deviation in any of these, we would all be dead. Can anybody believe this happened by chance? Only the stiff-necked intelligentsia!

If we consider the human body, their case only gets worse. The things that can go wrong in the body are without number. How come the bones are just the right size and length; the muscles the same; the nerves just right to go to every part, carrying messages to the brain from the senses to every other part; the blood just right for carrying food and oxygen; the heart just right for pumping; the veins, arteries and capillaries just right to reach every cell; the stomach, gallbladder and pancreas, just right to digest food; the lungs just right to pick up oxygen and exhale carbon dioxide; the glands just right for special effects; and the senses (eyes, ears, etc.), just right to pick up sight, sound, smell, taste and feeling? This is a question intelligentsia refuses to even look at. I know what they're like. I've had more than one professor heap scorn on me for even mentioning the creation story. I know for a fact that God will heap scorn on them in due time for believing and promoting such nonsense. He says so in Psalm 2, *"He that sits in the heavens shall laugh at them. The Lord shall have them in derision* (utter contempt)." Just a cursory look at the facts of life, the exquisite design, the perfect precision, the wonder of it all, should cause them and everyone else to bow down in humble adoration. *"The invisible things of God, from the creation of the world, are seen being understood by the things that are made, even His existence and power. They are without excuse and so God gave them up to vain* (empty) *imagination."* (Romans 1:20)

Life is the big conundrum. Where did it come from? They don't even want to guess. A big bang went off and presto, a living cell appeared and gradually developed into two cells, then three and kept going until there were millions of them joining together to make some simple forms of life, say worms, which then advanced to the monkey, and finally to the crown of evolution, a human being, with a brain and a soul, willpower, emotions, imagination, and even a conscience. Evolutionists believe things are evolving always for the better. So, what is next for man? They don't know, but hope for some kind of Superman. Unknowingly, they are right in one sense, the true sense, the Spiritual sense! God is producing a new race of people. They will be just like His Son, Jesus, and they will inherit the earth! (Romans 8:29) The scoffers should read Psalm 2:10-12, *"O you big shots, listen while there is time, fall down and worship God before His anger is aroused and you perish."*

## Death

Death is really an intruder in this world. God made the earth a place to live. Satan made it a place to die. It went from a garden to a cemetery. God gave our first parents a stern warning, "Stay away from the tree of the knowledge of good and evil on penalty of death." Adam deliberately disobeyed God and brought death to himself and to all his posterity. We know, since he didn't die right away physically, that there are two deaths; spiritual and physical. Adam died spiritually the day he disobeyed. This was a cutting of his ties to God, and the yielding of himself to Satan. From then on, his existence, and ours, in the world would be under a curse. Even the world would be under the curse. His physical life span would be cut short. Eventually he would die, and the body and soul would separate. From that day to now, people are born into this world dead, which sounds strange, but we are born spiritually cut off from God. *"By one man, sin entered the world and death by sin, and so death passed upon all men, for all have sinned."* (Romans 5:12) This is why we must be born again, getting back spiritually into the favor of God.

Fortunately for us, God so loved us that He was willing to pay the price to provide us with a new birth, which includes the gift of everlasting life, meaning we're saved from hell. It would be wonderful if this was a done deal for all people, but it's not. It's only for those who ask. God gave us the freedom to choose whom we will serve. If we choose not to go with God, we remain servants of Satan and will end up in hell with him. *"He that believes on the Son has everlasting life. He that believes not shall not see life, but the wrath of God abides on him."* (John 3:36)

For those who accept God's plan of salvation, their whole outlook on life and death changes. Death is no longer something to dread. The Apostle Paul said, *"We look forward to our heavenly bodies, realizing that time spent in these earthly bodies is time spent away from our eternal home - we are content to die, for then we will be at home with the Lord."* (2 Corinthians 5:6-8) *"I long to go and be with Christ. How much happier for me than being here."* (Philippians 1:23) *"For me to live is Christ, to die is gain."* (Philippians 1:21) *"God will open wide the gates of heaven for you."* (2 Peter 1:11) *"Precious in the sight of the Lord is the death of his saints."* (Psalm 116:15) *"Blessed be God - who has given us the privilege of being born again, so that we are now members of God's own family, having the priceless gift of eternal life."* (1 Peter 1:3-4)

I must point out a trap that Satan sets for every one of us: the fear of dying. Fear is a sure indicator of a weak faith or no faith at all.

We read in 2 Timothy 1:7, *"God has not given us the spirit of fear, but the spirit of power."* If you are lacking power, you need to spend time with the Lord, in the closet, until you know that you know, and nothing can shake you, not even the words that you have a month to live. With that kind of faith, you can say with Paul, *"O death where is thy sting? O grave where is thy victory? The sting of death is sin - but thanks be to God which gives us the victory through our Lord Jesus Christ."* (1 Corinthians 15:55)

## Death Conquered

*"O death, where is thy sting? O grave, where is thy victory? God gives us the victory through our Lord Jesus Christ."* (1 Corinthians 15:55- 57)

This has to be the best news ever heard. Hebrews 2:15 says, *"Jesus delivered those who, through fear of death, have been living all their lives as slaves to constant dread."* (Living Bible) There is no doubt that death is enemy number one. We do everything possible to delay it, to avoid it, and when it happens, to package it so it doesn't seem so bad, at least to the survivors.

How does Jesus deliver us from death? First, we need to understand that there are two deaths, physical and spiritual. When Adam sinned, he died spiritually, immediately being cut off from God. His body was sentenced to death at the same time, but it was delayed for many years to give him time to change his mind. If he repented of his sin, and turned back to the Lord, he would be recovered to the Lord and the spiritual death sentence would be cancelled. The physical death sentence would still be in effect, but if he remained faithful to the Lord, he would not experience the second eternal death. *"He that overcomes shall not be hurt of the second death."* (Revelation 2:11)

From the above, you can see that our main concern is to overcome and escape the second death. You will say only Christ can conquer death. Of course, Christ does it all for us, but only as we cooperate with Him. The first thing to do, if not saved, is to be born again (John 3:3). With this experience, we pass from death to life (John 5:29). The next thing is to devour the Word as a starving baby devours milk. (1 Peter 2:2 and John 6:51) With the knowledge and understanding we get from the Bible, we are ready to take on the enemy of our souls. Believe it or not (I say this because most people refuse to believe it), we must overcome Satan. Seven times in Revelation 2 and 3 we are told that to escape the second death, we must overcome. There's no escaping it. Then the question becomes, how do we overcome? We must be persuaded to leave no stone unturned in our determination to overcome Satan and win the prize of God's, "Well done."

The parable of the ten virgins is a graphic picture of people who left some stones unturned. (Matthew 25:1-13) They were all ready with their lamps, waiting for the coming of Christ. Five of them were foolish; taking no oil, the symbol of the Holy Spirit, with them. Suddenly He came, and they all went out to meet Him. The five who had no oil rushed to the store to buy some, but when they came back, they were too late. The door was shut. There's no way to describe the grief, the agony, the dashed hopes, the tears, and the inconsolable state of those who miss the coming of Christ, especially to be that close to being ready. The Bible says there will be weeping and gnashing of teeth. (Matthew 22:13 & 24:51)

Paul expresses the determination we need. He said, *"I run straight to the goal with purpose in every step. I fight to win. I punish my body, making it do what it should, not what it wants to - lest I should be a castaway."* (1 Corinthians 9:25-27) *"I count everything worthless, compared to the priceless gain of knowing Christ. So, whatever it takes, I will be one of those who are alive from the dead* (that is, escaping the second death)." (Philippians 3:8-11) This is the attitude that will overcome Satan and escape the second death. *"He that overcometh shall inherit all things."* (Revelation 21:7)

## Disasters

Are natural disasters punishment for ungodly people? Most people would say no. They have been taught, and they like to think, that God is a God of love. Sadly, this is only half the story. He is the God of love, but also the God of justice. "The soul that sins must die." That's a law like gravity. It can't be changed. The only reason God can forgive sin is because Jesus took our sin and our death penalty. If we refuse His offer of forgiveness, then we must die for our sins, and that's a disaster.

The Bible is full of illustrations of this law. In Luke 13:4, Jesus is telling His followers about a tower that fell and killed eighteen people. He asked them, "Do you think they were really bad sinners?" He said, "No, everybody is going to perish unless they repent." In other words, we're all in the same boat. We're sinners scheduled to die. This is a law that can't be broken. Every soul that sins must die and go to the wrong place unless he repents. The World Trade Center tragedy took 3000 souls away. But they were all sitting on death row. They just went prematurely. The real disaster is to die and go to the wrong place. Sin is the cause of all disasters, and especially, the eternal ones.

Most people think this life is all there is, so make the best of it. Get the best education, the best career, the best success, mansion, cars, boats, etc. If they could just get a grip on one word, they'd do an immediate about face. That word is 'temporary'. Our time on earth isn't even a drop in the ocean compared to eternity.

Following the story of the tower, Jesus told of a man that planted a fig tree and waited three years for fruit. Finding none, he said, "Cut it down. It's useless." This is a picture of us. If we don't produce the kind of good living, or fruit of the Spirit, then we're useless, worthless. Whether we're taken away by a disaster or by natural causes doesn't matter. The only thing that matters is whether we repent or not. Without repentance, we're doomed.

*"Except you repent, you shall all perish."* (Luke 13:5)

## Discipleship

After you are born again, you are soon faced with a choice to make: should you become a disciple or not? You will run into a verse like Matthew 16:24, *"If any man will come after me, let him deny himself, take up his cross and follow me."* The 'if' tells you it's not a requirement, it's a choice. You may be thinking we can't be disciples anyway. There were only 12 of them. But as you read the book of Acts, you see the first Christians were all called disciples. Later, they were called Christians. See Acts 11:26, *"The disciples were called Christians first in Antioch."*

Disciple is the same word as discipline. It means being under discipline, one who has made a commitment. You've heard of 'card carrying communists.' They were the 100% dedicated ones. Disciples are like that. They feel the tug of the Spiritual life. The super religious Pharisees looked Jesus over, but didn't feel that tug, and so they rejected Him. But one felt the tug. Nicodemus had to find out for himself, and he became one of God's disciples.

In Matthew 13:23, Jesus told a parable that illustrates the different levels of commitment, or interest. He explained that a sower sows seed; some in good soil and some in bad. Bad soil produces nothing. Good soil produces different amounts, some 30%, some 60%, and some 100%. He explained that the seed is God's Word, the bad soil represents people who have no time for God, and the good soil represents people who receive the Word and study it. (Psalm 1) These people will soon produce fruit. The fruit is the love, joy, peace, etc., of Galatians 5:22. It could also be the winning of souls. The different amounts of fruit are determined by the choices people make. The choices are determined by their commitment. For example, a new Christian would probably find it very difficult to love his enemy, but if he is wholly dedicated to the Lord, he will make more of an effort than a less dedicated Christian would make. The real test of commitment is the words of Jesus in John 8:31, "*If you continue in my Word, then you are my disciple indeed.*"

Another illustration of the different levels of the Christian life is found in Matthew 25:14. A businessman gave his servants different amounts of money and told them to trade and make a profit. Later when he checked with them, he rewarded them according to the amount they earned. In other words, your commitment determines your reward. All this should motivate us to be 100% disciples, but it's not easy. Remember the rich young ruler. He wanted to follow Jesus until he heard Jesus say, "*Sell everything you have and then follow me.*" He went away sorrowful.

Jesus, of course, knew that picking 12 disciples was a critical decision he had to make. Luke 6:13 says Jesus spent all night in prayer and in the morning, he picked them out of the crowd. Were they all perfect? No. Jesus saw not their intelligence or aptitude, but their hunger and thirst for righteousness. (Matthew 5:6) They were all on different levels of commitment, but all had that heart hunger. Peter, James, and John turned out to be the most committed, since they became his inner circle. John was the most favored, even being called the disciple that Jesus loved. (John 13:23) As each one was called, he immediately left all his own interests and followed Jesus, staying the course for three years. It's an illustration of Matthew 20:16, "*Many are called, but only a few are chosen.*" We wonder how many in our churches today would have been chosen. And what about us? Would we have been chosen? Did the disciples make mistakes? Yes, in fact, a glaringly bad mistake, when at the Garden of Gethsemane, they all forsook him and fled. (Matthew 26:56) Were they forgiven? Yes. (1 John 1:9) Was their sacrifice worth it all? They weren't too sure. The disciples wondered as any normal person would, "What am I getting out of this?" Peter said, "*We have left all and followed you.*" Jesus said, "There is no one who has denied himself who shall not receive manifold more in this life, and in the world to come, life everlasting." (Luke 18:28 paraphrased) A little later, the Apostle Paul would say, "*Eye has not seen nor ear heard, what God has prepared for them that love Him.*" (1 Corinthians 2:9) In the end, all the disciples, except Judas, remained faithful unto death.

## Drink or Die

For over 90 years, I've prided myself in never spending a night in the hospital. I've been there a few times but didn't have to stay. That almost changed back in October 2007. I'd been feeling weak and dizzy for a few days, but when I could hardly make it to the kitchen, I agreed I needed help. With a lot of effort and assistance, I got into the car. At the hospital, a man put me in a wheelchair and took me to a bed on wheels. Another person wheeled me to a room. Yet another came, asked questions, and put stickers all over me for a test. A doctor came and looked at the test results on the screen, asked more questions, and left. An hour later, the doctor came again, and took some more tests. Later the Chief Doctor came in and broke the news to me: "You are dehydrated!" I had never heard of such a thing. They hooked me up to a bag of saline solution. About two hours later, they said it was my choice to stay or go home. I chose to go home and was soon back in bed, feeling slightly better, but not well enough to stay up. The next day I felt even better, but still stayed in bed. It's unbelievable to me that drinking water could be so important to health, but for a while at least I'm going to force myself to drink, if just to see if they're right. I must admit, five doctors saying the same thing - "drink or die" - got my attention. I am following their advice and am feeling some better. Praise the Lord.

The fact that physical water is so important certainly reminds me of all the references to water in the Bible. If physical water is important, spiritual water is much more important, as shown in the following verses:

After leaving Egypt, Israel ran out of water, and they complained loudly. (Exodus 17:6) Moses was commanded to strike a rock and it would yield water. The rock represents Jesus. The striking would be the crucifixion, and the water would be spiritual life. Later, Israel again lacked water and God told Moses to speak to the rock. Moses was angry at the time and struck the rock. For this disobedience, he was deprived of the honor of leading Israel into the Promised Land. The lesson was that Christ, the Rock, would be crucified once for our salvation and it was not necessary to be crucified again. (Hebrews 9:26 and 10:12)

In Numbers 8:7, the Lord told Moses to set the Levites apart from the other tribes to serve in the Tabernacle. He did this by sprinkling water of purification upon them. In Ephesians 5:26, we read, "*Christ loved the church and gave himself for it that He might sanctify and cleanse it with the washing of water by the Word.*" In these verses, water stands for the Word of God. Do we want to be set apart for God's service, cleansed of all sin? Be in the Word!

Isaiah 12:3 says, "*O, the joy of drinking deeply from the fountain of salvation.*" In Isaiah 55:1, we read, "*Ho, everyone that thirsts come to the waters.*" In John 7:37, Jesus said, "*If anyone is thirsty let him come to me and drink. Rivers of living water shall flow from him. This spake He of the Spirit which they that believe on Him shall receive.*"

In Revelation 22:1, John said, "*God showed me a pure river of the water of life - proceeding out of the throne of God and of the Lamb*" and in verse 17, "*Whosoever will, let him take the water of life freely.*" Revelation 21:6 says, "*I will give to him that is thirsty of the fountain of the Word of Life freely.*"

I take from all these verses that water is an object lesson to show us how important the Word of God is. Just as water is essential for physical life, so the Word of God is essential for spiritual life. Because I neglected drinking water, I nearly died. How important then is it that we drink our full measure of the living water, the Word of God. Granted, there are Christians that don't get in the Word. Paul says in 1 Corinthians 3:1, *"You are still spiritual babies. I have to feed you with milk."* Verse 15 says, *"they will be saved as by fire."* It's a chance I wouldn't take.

## Drowning

I used to be a lifeguard, and I know what it's like to be caught in an undertow, and how desperate a person feels when going down for the last time. If anything or anybody is near enough, he will grab it with a death grip. In our training for the job, we had to know how to break the death grip of a drowning person. In the final test, we had to rescue a big burly lifeguard captain who grabbed us around the neck and locked his arms. We went right to the bottom and stayed there until we broke his grip, or he could see that we weren't up to it. Then he mercifully let us go. I can tell you it was a hairy experience and I'm telling it to help you understand that spiritually, we all are in a drowning situation.

Satan, the ugliest creature of all, has a death grip on us and there's no escaping unless you know what to do, and don't look for mercy from him. You ask, "What are we drowning in?" Ah, the question shows you're half drowned already. The answer is found in 1 John 2:15, *"Love not the world, neither the things that are in the world. If anyone loves the world, the love of the Father is not in him."* In Luke 4:6, Satan says, *"The world is mine and I give it to whoever I please."* 1 John 2:16 says, *"All that is in the world, the lust of the flesh, the lust of the eyes and the pride of life* (ego) *is of Satan."* We might as well face the fact, we are all drowning in a sea of wickedness. Martin Luther said this in 'A Mighty Fortress', "We're all in a flood of mortal ills prevailing." We are drowning because we've allowed Satan to get a grip on us with these three lusts. Who among us can say they are free of lusts?

The point of this article is that there is a way to break Satan's grip, but few people know what it is and even the people that know, don't always use it. Eve knew better, but she was caught flat-footed. She saw that the tree was good for food (lust of the flesh), pleasing to the eye (lust of the eye) and would make her wise (ego; pride). Satan had his death grip on her, and she went right to the bottom, and took the whole race with her.

Jesus was tempted in the same manner. "*Make bread for yourself* (lust of the flesh). *Look at the glamorous world. Serve me and I'll give it to you* (lust of the eyes). *Throw yourself off the temple. Show the people your power* (lust of ego)." Jesus knew how to break Satan's death grip. He used the Sword of the Spirit, "*It is written --.*" Satan had to let go. This is the Lord's gift to us; the secret of overcoming Satan. Just as someone was kind enough to teach me how to break a physical grip, Jesus is teaching us how to break a Satanic grip. Here it is again for those that missed it: You must use the Sword of the Spirit. That, of course, means you must memorize the Bible verses that deal with temptation. They used to have Sword drills for children, but it was just knowing where a verse was found. The Sword drill we should have is calling out a temptation and coming up with the right counter-verse. Jesus had the right answer for three temptations, not by luck, but by study. The problem is, most people can't be bothered memorizing scripture, let alone learning how to use them.

I hope everyone who reads this will recognize the danger we're in when we desire more and more things for our comfort, more and more things for our viewing pleasure (TV), and more and more things to make us proud. Be ready with a good verse when you see Satan coming with these temptations.

# Elite

Most of us don't like the idea of an inner circle, or an elite group of people. It suggests snobbery, 'better than you', etc. Job, in exasperation at his three 'friends', said, "No doubt you are the people, wisdom shall die with you, but I have understanding too." We've all felt that way at some time. In my long life, I've seen plenty.

However, much as we dislike it, elitism is a fact of life, and believe it or not, it's very big in the Bible. Just to cite a few examples, the twelve sons of Jacob, though deeply flawed, were honored, not only in this life, but in the New Jerusalem. Their names are written on the twelve gates. (Revelation 21:12) The twelve disciples were also especially favored. Their names are on the foundation of the New Jerusalem. (Revelation 21:14) Among the twelve sons of Jacob, Joseph was the most favored. Among the twelve disciples, John was the most favored. Among the disciples, three were favored more than the rest. Several times, Jesus showed His preference for Peter, James, and John. (See Luke 8:51, 9:28 and Matthew 26:37)

In the Old Testament, God often referred to His special friends as the remnant. The word means something left over, probably useless, but it came to mean survivor. Isaiah 1:9 says, "*Except the Lord had left unto us a very small remnant, we should have been as Sodom and Gomorrah.*" Isaiah 10:20 says, "*The remnant that escaped shall return to God.*" It came to mean God's chosen ones. It began with Abraham and his family, later called Israel. They were chosen out of the mass of wicked people, but they themselves were a mixed multitude. "*A mixed multitude went with them.*" (Exodus 12:38) "*The mixed multitude fell to lusting.*" (Numbers 11:4) As time went on, the remnant became smaller and smaller. Elijah, at one time, thought he was the only faithful one left, but God said, "*No, I have a remnant of 7,000 that haven't bowed to Baal* (an idol)."

To God, that small remnant was the elite. Jesus said, "*Many are called, few are chosen.*" (Matthew 20:16 and 22:14) Being a part of the elite is an option open to all, but only a few respond. Today, if you say you are one of God's chosen few, a lot of Christians will look at you with disdain and call you an elitist. "We're all children of God," they say. One church I know had a split. The group leaving called themselves the remnant, which of course meant to many Christians they were elitists. There will be a separation on judgment day, and then all will see who the elitists are.

*"The whole creation is watching with eager expectancy of the revealing of the sons of God."* (Romans 8:19)

## Esau and Jacob

In Genesis 32, there is a beautiful story of two brothers, mortal enemies who were reconciled. Jacob cheated his brother, Esau, two times: out of his birthright and his inheritance. That was serious stuff and Jacob ran away. After many years, the Lord told him to return home. He was hoping Esau had forgotten, or at least mellowed. Suddenly, he was faced with a crisis. His brother, Esau, was coming to meet him with 400 men. This could only mean one thing. He was coming to kill him and his whole family. Jacob was in a panic. He divided his family and told them to go in opposite directions; so hopefully, at least half would be saved. Then he went off by himself to seek God. The Bible describes him as wrestling all night with a man. (Genesis 32:24) Jacob said to the man, *"I will not let you go until you bless me."* The man, which had to be God, was so pleased with Jacob's perseverance that He said, *"You shall no more be called Jacob* (deceiver), *but Israel,* (prince or son of God), *for as a prince you have power with God and with men and have prevailed."* Jacob was overwhelmed and said, *"I have seen God face to face."* That morning, Esau also was changed. Instead of killing Jacob and his family, he ran to meet him, embraced him, kissed him, and they both wept. What a change!

This wonderful story has plenty of meaning for us. The first one I see is that God worked a mighty miracle in answer to serious prayer. Esau had, for years, been looking forward to the time he could get revenge on Jacob. He didn't come with 400 men to have a picnic. That God could turn that hatred into love, should encourage us to pray harder. Jacob prayed all night. It was probably the first time he had ever gotten serious with God. Seeking God earnestly and fervently is a rare thing. How do I know? Because God works wonders when we get serious. *"The eyes of the Lord run everywhere to show Himself strong on behalf of them whose heart is perfect toward Him."* (2 Chronicles 16:9) God is looking for opportunities to work miracles. Since we don't see many miracles, we can deduce there isn't much serious praying going on. It takes a crisis to drive us to our knees and change us from half committed to wholly committed.

The second thing I see is that Jacob, the deceiver, received a great promotion. He had some sort of relationship with God, but he was still a deceiver and not a son of God until this crisis came. Maybe we should pray for a crisis in our lives so that we can experience that kind of a change! I know some think all saved people are sons of God, but the Bible says, *"As many as are led by the Spirit, they are the sons of God."* (Romans 8:14) All saved people are not being led by the Spirit. We also see Paul exhorting his people to grow up. He told them they were still babies. (1 Corinthians 3:1) A baby may be in the family, but he's not considered a son in the Biblical sense.

The third thing I see is that God doesn't need our help. Jacob sent messengers to Esau to placate him, but they returned and told Jacob that Esau was on his way to meet him with 400 men. Jacob realized that only God could help him. I have friends and relatives that are unsaved, and invariably, I think I must change them with my witnessing, which sometimes becomes an argument. I can see, we should direct all our energies toward seeking God. He tells us this in 2 Chronicles 7:14, *"If my people will humble themselves and seek my face – I will hear – and forgive – and heal."*

61

There are more meanings here I'm sure, but these three could make a big difference in our lives.

## Face the Facts

This world has some incontrovertible facts. One is that we're going to die. Another is that we're all sinners. And another is that there's going to be a judgment day.

Looking back at a long life, I thought I was good at facing the facts, but they were mostly little problems that I could handle. I either made the right decisions or muddled through, someway. Today, at age 90, I'm looking at a fact that can't be sidestepped. I'm at the end of the line. I notice lately the aging process is accelerating. I used to do 20 pushups. After a long time, I settled for 15, another long time 10, then it speeded up until the day came I didn't even want to think about them. They are out of my life for good. In departing, they left me a message: "Get your house in order. You're out of here yourself pretty soon." Well, that's an undeniable fact. I haven't been there before and all the trillions of people that have been there aren't talking. Maybe what happens is they start thinking about it and poof, they're gone. Well, if I get to finish this article, here's what I think:

To be ready for the inevitable, we need to get the facts and face them - do something about them. Martin Luther was facing death and he put his thoughts into the song, "A Mighty Fortress is Our God." He said, "Let goods and kindred go." That's what we must do all right, but truth to tell, we never should have gotten attached to goods and the like in the first place. This life is not the real life. It is just temporary to see who wants to qualify for the true life in heaven. Jesus said, "*If you love father or mother more than me, you're not worthy of me.*" (Matthew 10:37) Paul said, "*I have suffered the loss of all things for Christ.*" (Philippians 3:8) In Philippians 1:23 Paul says, "*I have a desire to depart and be with Christ.*" Let's make sure goods and the like have no death grip on us.

A second fact Luther faced in his song: "Though this world is filled with devils trying to kill me, I will not fear." Sadly, most people don't even know there's a war going on, but it's a fact, Satan and his devils are out to get us. Jesus said, *"Satan comes to steal, kill, and destroy."* (John 10:10) But Luther said, "I tremble not for him. His rage I can endure, for lo his doom is sure. One little word shall fell him." That word is Jesus. There's no excuse for the Christian to live in fear or defeat. Let's use God's Word, the Sword of the Spirit, to put Satan and his devils to flight. He's a defeated foe, and we should always be on the victorious side. For the unbeliever, you might have been a sinner all your life, but you can be saved. The Bible says, *"Whosoever shall call upon the name of the Lord shall be saved."* (Romans 10:13) How does it work? Just do the following:

A.  Admit (acknowledge) you're a sinner and ask Jesus to forgive you.
B.  Believe that Jesus is the Son of God. *"For God so loved the world, He gave his only begotten Son, that whosoever believes in Him should not perish, but have everlasting life."* (John 3:1)
C.  Confess your conversion. *"With the mouth confession is made unto salvation."* (Romans 10:10)

If you do these three things in sincerity, you will be saved. That's a fact you need to embrace.

The fourth fact in Luther's song is that we don't get saved to escape hell. "God has willed His truth to triumph through us." God's first man, Adam, failed the test and doomed all his descendants to the curse of sin, death, and hell. God's second man, Jesus, passed the test and blessed all true believers with righteousness, life, and heaven. If we are truly saved and continue to follow Jesus, we will hear God say, "Well done good and faithful servant." God's truth will triumph, and, by his grace, it will be through us.

# Fellowship

There are many levels of fellowship. A mother has fellowship with her baby, but it is very elementary. As the baby grows, the fellowship increases until the child becomes an adult. All the time the child is growing, fellowship is fluctuating. There are times when fellowship is sweet and times when it is sour. I remember times, as a boy, I wouldn't speak to my Mom. We had a serious disagreement once about going to the movies. All the kids were going and, to me, it was a matter of life and death. I almost literally died having to stay home and miss the fun. Another time, a friend's mother died. I was so shaken up thinking of what would happen to me if Mom died that I had very good fellowship for quite a while.

Affinity groups have a certain level of fellowship. They could be related by hobbies, clubs, work, school, etc. They have a common bond that unites them. Marriage, of course, should have a very high level of fellowship. The highest level of fellowship is Spiritual. Having the same Father, serving the same Master, listening to the same voice, reading the same letters, studying the same history, worshiping the same Lord, all adds up to, as they say today, being on the same page. But even in such a close family, there are many levels. Jesus had twelve disciples. They were certainly a close-knit group, but each one related to each other and to Jesus on a different level. The obvious example is the spread from Judas, the betrayer, to John, the beloved. A second obvious example is the way Jesus favored Peter, James, and John. He took them up to the Mount of Transfiguration and with Him to pray in Gethsemane. Most Bible scholars say that Jesus had the closest fellowship with John. At the last supper, John was leaning on Jesus. He was called the disciple Jesus loved. (John 13:23)

The key ingredient to close fellowship is agreement. When two people agree, fellowship is sweet. The greater the importance of the subject of agreement, the greater the fellowship. To agree about a ball game is shallow. To agree that Jesus is Lord is true fellowship. To agree that absolute surrender to Jesus is the only way to live is heartfelt fellowship. It would be like a perfect marriage, of which there are too few!

For those who desire such a wonderful fellowship, there is only one way: spend time with the Lord in the Word, in prayer, and in church. The better you know Jesus, the more you'll agree with Him. The more you agree, the closer you'll become. The closer you become, the better the fellowship. To be very specific, five minutes or even one or two hours won't do it. Paul said, *"Pray without ceasing."* He said, *"Let the Word of God dwell in you richly."* (1 Thessalonians 5:17 and Colossians 3:16) Think back to your courtship days. You spent as much time as possible with your friend. If you had serious intentions, you agreed with everything your friend said (at least until after the honeymoon).

Jesus said, *"A new command I give you that you love one another as I have loved you. By this shall all men know that you are my disciples."* (John 13:34 & 35) The early church realized this ideal. They even had true communion for a while where they pooled their resources to spread the gospel. Then Ananias and Saphira sinned and ruined it. (Acts 5:1) Today, every fellowship is a mixed bag. The best we can hope for, in these last days, is two or three like-minded people. Jesus said where two or three gather in His name, He is there.

## Finders Keepers

I remember as a boy hearing this rhyme many times, "Finders keepers, losers weepers." I remember, it was a fact of life. If you lost something and someone found it, you were out of luck, as far as getting it back.

The idea of finding and losing is quite prominent in the Bible. Just to mention a few; a man found a treasure in a field, a pearl merchant found an outstanding pearl, a woman lost a coin, the shepherd lost his sheep. Each incident has an important application for us, but now we will look at another case of lost and found.

This one is very much overlooked or ignored. Jesus said in Matthew 10:39, *"He that finds his life shall lose it, and he that loses his life for my sake, shall find it."* This is a conundrum that will take a little study. In the first phrase, the man finds life and then loses it. It seems obvious that there are two kinds of life in this world: false and true. The false life is characterized by that which pertains to the flesh or body activities, i.e., broad way of pleasure; eating, drinking, and being merry. How many people have been thrilled to be invited to some big party and think they have found the good life. But, it is all short-lived. All that glitters is not gold, and the person that pursues this path will lose everything. The best example of this situation is the prodigal son. He couldn't wait to enjoy the good life, but he ended up in a pig pen

The one that loses his life and finds it is the one that sees that life is more than a game. There is good and evil, life and death. There must be a reason for everything. He begins to seek for truth, reality, and God. He is glad to sacrifice temporary pleasures for something that will last. We read in Hebrews 11:26 that Moses chose to suffer affliction with the people of God rather than enjoy the pleasures of sin for a season, for he could see there was a reward up ahead. Jesus sounded the warning. The broad way leads to destruction. The narrow way leads to life. Therefore, choose life.

Jim Elliott, a missionary to the Auca Indians in South America, was killed by the people he came to save. Later, they found this sentence in his writings: "That man is no fool who gives up what he can't keep for something that he can't lose."

## First Love

When all's said and done, our strivings for prosperity, knowledge, understanding, prestige, power, influence, achievements, benefits, comfort, security, growth, our desire for a closer walk, fuller dedication, acceptable service, greater faith, more fruit, more holiness, better ministry, more zeal, etc., etc.; when all these things are achieved, only one thing counts, and that is obeying the first and greatest command, *"Thou shall love the Lord thy God with all thy heart, soul and mind."* (Matthew 22:36)

That one test will seal you in or seal you out of God's Kingdom. In Revelations, the last book of the Bible, the one that sums up all things, we read these words, *"I have something against you. You have left your first love."* (2:4) *"You are lukewarm."* (3:16) In the love chapter, 1 Corinthians 13, we read, *"You can be perfect, even be burned alive for preaching the gospel, but without love, it profits nothing."* (John 4:23) The truth is that God doesn't want anything from us but our love. In John 13:35, Jesus says, *"By love shall all men know you are my disciples."*

In Luke 7:36-50, there is the story of Jesus going to Simon's house for dinner. A sinful woman came in and began to wash Jesus' feet. Simon, in his heart, began to criticize Jesus for accepting love from a sinner. Then Jesus let him have it. He said, "I came to visit you and you offered me no kiss, no water to wash my feet, and no oil to anoint my head. This woman has shown me much love. You have shown me none." Poor Simon must have been mortified. How about us? When we invite Jesus to sup with us, (in the secret closet), are we like Simon, withholding any expression of love? Do we just come with requests for favors?

Only one disciple was known for his love, John, called the beloved. He always got as close to Jesus as possible. When they arrested Jesus, all the disciples fled, except John. As he stood under the cross, Jesus asked him to take care of His mother. What a reward!

Later, John was honored in writing one of the most wonderful books in the world, the Gospel of John. Peter was a wonderful disciple, but Jesus had to ask him three times if he loved Him. Peter, of course, did, but the problem was, he didn't show it.

Jesus despises the lukewarm. He said He'd spit them out of His mouth - not a pretty picture. One of the great poets, John Milton, said that giving faint (weak) praises for a great achievement is an insult. Try to imagine Babe Ruth hitting a homerun and winning the World Series, and the fans politely clapping their hands. The sports world and the media would never stop talking about it. It's just too far out, stupid, and abnormal! But what's winning a ball game compared to what Jesus did for us and for the whole world. Are we giving Him faint praise?

We need to see Him suffering for us. How do we respond to Jesus taking the nails in His hands that were marked for our hands? This is the truth that will change us. Paul saw it and said, *"I am determined to know nothing save Jesus Christ and Him crucified."* (1Corinthians 2:2) He was consumed with one thought: Jesus suffered in his place. The Psalmist said, *"I will bless the Lord at all times. His praise will be in my mouth continually."* (Psalm 34:1) *"All that is within me bless the Lord."* (Psalm 103:1) William Booth of the Salvation Army said, "Jesus has every bit of me." That sounds like the kind of love we need to have - the kind that will result in God saying, *"This is my beloved son (or daughter) in whom I am well pleased."*

## Fruit

Every fruit of a tree: apples, oranges, etc., is programmed to be a full-grown, sweet, desirable, and tasty treat. An apple or orange that doesn't reach this stage will be cast out as worthless. The process of growing from its inception to its full ripeness takes time and work. There are nutrients that must be absorbed, as well as water and sunlight. There are also enemies that must be fought: insects, worms, etc. But when everything works together for good, that apple or peach will win the approval of the inspectors. It will have progressed from an insignificant seed to a dessert fit for a king.

This is the story of God's people. We are insignificant as seeds, but "*When the corn of wheat* (that's us) *falls into the ground and dies* (takes up the cross), *it brings forth much fruit.*" (John 12:24) The seed dies, making way for a new thing to start to live. It is the new life, the new nature, a godly person. This new life, just like the plant, must have water (the Word of God), sunlight (the Holy Spirit), and must have protection. All this is provided by God. Just as the tree endures the cold winter, the storms, and the blights, the new life must endure the trials and temptations. It is on its way to providing God a special treat. What is the way? In the words of a chorus: "Shut in with God in the secret place, there in the Spirit beholding His face, gaining new power to run in the race; O, I want to be shut in with God." God gives us everything we need: the Bible, the Holy Spirit, the church, even protection from our enemies. In due time, He looks for fruit, the manifestation of a new creation (Ephesians 2:10, 2 Corinthians 5:17), for all the world to see (Ephesians 3:10). The fruit would be spiritual qualities like love, joy, peace, longsuffering, gentleness, goodness, faithfulness, meekness, and self-control. (Galatians 5:22) One of the scariest verses in the Bible is Mark 11:13-14. Jesus was hungry and when He saw a fig tree, He looked for figs, but saw only leaves. He cursed it and it died. John 15:2 5 says, "*Every branch in me* (the saved) *that bears not fruit, He takes away - he that abides in me brings forth much fruit.*" I notice in the creation story, the first thing God said to Adam and Eve was, "*Be fruitful.*" (Genesis 1:28) In the famous first Psalm, we read, "*A good man brings forth fruit in its season.*" The verse before this one says, "*The good man meditates in the Word day and night.*" Another scary verse is John 15:16, "*I have ordained you to bring forth fruit.*" Some people think that's just for the preacher. Oh no, He's talking to all of us. "*Abide in me and I in you. The branch cannot bear fruit except it abides in the vine. If a man abides not in me - he is cast into the fire.*" (John 15:4 & 6)

Hebrews 13:15 says, *"By Him therefore, let us offer the sacrifice of praise to God continually,"* i.e., the fruit of our lips giving thanks to Him. Did you realize that words are fruit? That's one fruit that everybody can produce. The Psalms are full of praise. Psalm 34:1 says, *"I will bless the Lord at all times, His praise will be in my mouth continually. O, magnify the Lord with me. Let us exalt His name together."* Revelation 22:2 says, *"There (in heaven) was the tree of life which bore twelve manner of fruits and yielded her fruit every month."* It seems clear that the Bible gives fruit bearing a much higher priority than most of us do. We still have time, as long as we are breathing. There's a song that says, "God is so wonderful, I can't explain, but I can say, glory, hallelujah, praise His Holy Name." At least, let us give Him thanks and praise!

## Galileo

Romans 1:20 says, *"That which may be known of God is manifest,* (clearly seen), *being understood by the things which He made. The invisible things of God are understood by the visible things."* Anyone that refuses to acknowledge God is without excuse and will pay a great price for their arrogance.

God has made many things to help us understand what He is like. Some are obvious, some are not, some require much thought, some are small, and some are large. The one we will look at is very large. It is the discovery by Galileo concerning the movements of the sun and earth. I like this one because it proved that the church leaders at that time were no better than other sinners. It was bad enough that worldly leaders should be evil and arrogant, but what can we say when church leaders are even worse?

Galileo, by careful study, discovered that the sun doesn't go around the earth, but the earth goes around the sun. This was unbelievable to everybody and especially to church leaders. Anybody could see that the sun was the one that was moving. Church leaders were incensed. They said, "This is heresy." They condemned Galileo and tried to kill him for suggesting such a wicked thing. In those days, if you disagreed with the church, you were very likely to be killed. Well, of course, Galileo was proved right, which should have caused the church leaders to realize they were not as infallible as they claimed to be, but it made no impression on them.

All of us are born thinking we are the center of the universe. Most people live out their whole lives under this delusion. It's me first. Self is the center of all thoughts, words, and actions. God, and everyone else, revolves around the big me. It takes time and a miracle of God's grace to make us realize that we are not the center, and that God is the true center. God is not our bellhop, waiting to do our will. Rather, we should be revolving around Him, wanting to do His will. If we don't see this and don't take our proper position, we are in deep trouble. In the case of the earth and the sun, there are no great consequences for those who don't understand it. Their mistaken idea doesn't really hurt anybody. But if an individual clings to the idea that he is the center of everything, he is doomed. Unless Christ becomes the center of our lives, we are lost and bound for hell. In Galatians 2:20 Paul said, "*I am crucified with Christ, nevertheless I live, yet, not I, but Christ lives in me, and the life I now live in the flesh, I live by the faith of the Son of God who loved me and gave Himself for me.*" This verse is saying that self must be killed, deposed of, and replaced by Christ. Then and then only, is the 'rightful' order established where our whole lives revolve around Him.

## Get It Right

If you've ever worked for someone, and who hasn't, you've probably heard the title words. The implication is clear, there will be consequences. Get it right or else. Now think of this: of all the jobs in the world, only one is truly important. In fact, it is more important than all the others together. What is it? It's the job of preparing yourself to meet God, to stand before him on judgment day. This is the one thing you must get right. The consequences of getting this wrong are a trillion times more horrific than anything else. You can get everything else right, but if you fail to get ready for the judgment day, you're a loser, big time. Jesus said if you gain the whole world and lose your soul, what can you give to get it back? (Mark 8:36) The answer is nothing. You've lost it all.

Now, if you are smart, you are asking how do I get it right? The Bible has the answer. There are thousands of verses that tell you how to get it right. Are you willing to look at them? Are you willing to obey them? Let's just take one. In John chapter 3, verses 1 to 12, a man named Nicodemus came to Jesus with some questions. Being very religious, as far as the man knew, he was okay with the Lord, but he still wasn't 100% sure. He was a smart man. He knew that his most important job in this world was to get his soul right. Not taking any chances, or wanting to leave it up to somebody else or to some institution that had a vested interest in holding on to him, he said to Jesus, "I know you're from God, because of the miracles you do." Jesus said to him rather abruptly, "*You must be born again.*" He was completely baffled. All he could think of was physical birth and asked, "*Can I enter my mother's womb and be born a second time?*" Jesus said, "*Are you a religious leader and you don't know this?*" Nicodemus didn't say anything after that. He was speechless. I'm glad to say though, that Nicodemus was later converted, because he helped with the burial of Jesus. (John 19:39)

What did Jesus mean by saying we must be born again? He meant you must be changed from a flesh person (selfish, human nature) to a Holy Spirit person. (John 3:6) "*For to be carnally minded* (flesh) *is death; Spirit minded is life and peace.*" (Romans :6) If you do not experience the new birth, you are carnal and will die in your sins. "*It is the Spirit that makes alive. The flesh profits nothing.*" (John 6:63) How does it work? It works by faith. John 1:12 and 13 say, "*As many as received Him* (Jesus), *to them gave he the power* (authority) *to become the sons of God, which were born, not of blood* (of our parents), *nor of the will of the flesh* (your own doing), *nor of the will of man* (someone telling you what to do), *but of God*." You simply tell God you know you're a sinner, ask Him to forgive you, and tell Him you want to receive Jesus as your Savior. If you don't know why you should, then read the gospels. You receive Him in your heart by faith. How it works is a mystery. Jesus compared it to the wind. We don't know where it comes from or where it's going, but we know it's real. (John 3:8) When you're born of the Spirit, you desire Spiritual food, which is the Word of God. (1 Peter 2:2)

What does God require but that we be born again, be in the Word, be in prayer and live a Godly life. Back in Old Testament days, people had to do things, rituals, etc., to be saved. In New Testament days, we do things (good works) because we are saved. What's so hard about that? Luke 1:80 says, speaking of John the Baptist, "The child grew strong in the Spirit." We can say it is simple enough even for a child to understand. The weirdest thing about this whole scenario is that the most important thing in the world is almost totally ignored. Christians don't bother to warn people anymore and preachers don't preach it. It's like going to church and calling yourself a Christian is all there is to it. Jesus warned about this. He said, *"Many will say in that day, "Lord, Lord, we did this for you." He will say, "I never knew you."* (Matthew 7:22) They just didn't bother to get it right.

## God's Purpose

God's greatest creation is not our universe, with the earth, the stars, the galaxies, etc. It is the people He made to live here. His purpose was to have a family made in His image. (The same purpose married couples have.)

God made Adam and Eve. He gave them an easy test to see what they would be like. He said, *"Eat of all the trees except one."* Adam failed this test and immediately he felt guilty, shamed, remorseful, and dirty. He hid from his friend. Fellowship, trust, and pleasure were all gone. Fear came. He knew his creator could snuff Him out in a moment.

God's holiness and justice automatically condemns rebellion to instant death. Man died spiritually - cut off from his maker. But God's love also came into play. In His wisdom, He knew there was only one way to save His creature. He had to do the unthinkable. God, the Son, had to take man's place as a human being and then take the death penalty on Himself. *"He was slain from the foundation of the world."* (Revelation 13:8)

God accomplished this by the greatest object lesson ever devised. He took the Roman government, the best of all governments, and the Jewish religion, the best of all religions, and let them demonstrate for all time, the desperately wicked nature of man. They conspired together to nail the Son of God to a cross. They never realized that they were exposing their corruption or that they were serving God's purpose to kill man's substitute, the Lamb, that takes away the sins of the world!

Because of God's love, man has a pardon for sin and a new life in Christ, but here is the saddest part of the story. So many churchgoers think that all they need to do is join the church and they're saved. They need to know that salvation is like a check that must be cashed, or a contract that must be signed. It is a personal transaction. It is a relationship with the Lord, formed by a two-way conversation, Bible reading and prayer. Without this, man is just as lost as ever.

## Godly, Godless

The word godless is mostly used as a criticism, a note of disapproval, like saying, "They sure are a godless bunch." Originally, it meant they were pagans, infidels, or heathens; but it has come to mean they're uncivilized, or they're barbarians. The true meaning is obvious. A godless people are people that live without God. With that meaning in mind, we'd better confess we're all pretty much godless.

All we need to do is remember the first and greatest commandment, *"Thou shalt love the Lord thy God, with all thy heart, with all thy soul, with all thy strength, and with all thy mind."* (Luke 10:22) How many obey that commandment? Or remember Psalm 1, *"A godly man's delight is in the law of the Lord and in His law doth he meditate day and night."* Anybody doing that? I'm afraid we're all too busy. The world is our nemesis. We read in James 4:4, *"The friendship of the world is enmity with God. Whosoever will be a friend of the world is the enemy of God."* Romans 8:7 says, *"To be carnally* (worldly) *minded is to be the enemy of God."* Even back in Paul's day, worldly things had first claim. We fall short of the godly life. Going to church doesn't make one godly, even going two or three times a week. That only amounts to tipping our hat. It shows some respect for God, but it's what happens the rest of the week that counts.

Psalm 119:11 says, *"Thy Word have I hidden in my heart* (memorized) *that I might not sin against thee."* Does any Christian memorize scriptures? It isn't often you hear an exhortation to memorize Bible verses, yet that is probably one of the main ways to be godly.

A perfect description of a godly person is found in Matthew 5. They are poor in spirit (humble and knowing their shortcomings). They mourn (for the lost and blind). They are meek (the opposite of proud). They hunger and thirst for righteousness (more of God). They are merciful (kind and forgiving). They are pure in heart (reject every impure thought). They strive for peace (with themselves and with others). They are the salt of the earth, and they are the light of the world. Without them, this world would be a jungle. O, for more godly people.

## Growth and Development

I remember as a boy hearing church talk about people being shallow or deep. I didn't know what they were talking about then, but through the years, it dawned on me that Christianity is more than just joining a church. It's getting reborn spiritually and then growing the same as a physical baby, by nourishment and exercise, etc., and becoming a spiritual adult.

A deep Christian gets in the Word to understand God's plan as much as possible. A shallow Christian is satisfied to spend an hour a week in church. It's strange that most Christians settle for the shallow life. How can a person believe that Jesus died for them and not have any desire to know Him? But strangest of all is the fact that little or no interest in the Lord is considered normal. No one, least of all the ecclesiastical hierarchy, is concerned about it. They see people year in and year out remaining as spiritual babies.

Paul saw the problem of our growth and addressed it immediately. He said to the Corinthians, "*I could not speak to you as to spiritual, but as to babes. I have fed you with milk, not meat, for you are not able to bear it.*" (1 Corinthians 3:1 & 2) In Hebrews 5:12, "*You ought to be teachers, but you need someone to teach you the first lessons. You are unskilled in the Word of righteousness. You need to understand the deeper things of God's Word. Let's stop going over the same old ground again and again. Let us become mature in our understanding, not laying again the foundation of repentance from dead works and faith towards God, baptisms, laying on of hands, etc.*" Paul wanted people to move on from knowing how to be saved, to knowing why you were saved. Jesus didn't lose any time declaring the difference between being saved and moving on. To be saved, one only needs to receive Jesus as Savior. (John 1:12 & 3:16) Justification is by faith, but growth and development is by work. It's just the same as in the physical realm. You don't do anything to get born, but from then on, it's work. Sad to say, spiritual babies cry a lot, just as physical babies do. After Israel escaped from Egypt, being born, they did nothing but cry for over 40 years. Today it's the same. A newborn Christian has trouble, and right away, he questions God, or worse yet, he blames God.

Physical birth, growth, and development are given much more importance in our world than spiritual. If a child stops growing, action is taken. Specialists are called. It's the same with mental growth. Our school systems are determined to give everyone a good education. The federal government even got into it with their 'no child left behind' laws. Oh, that we had some leadership like that in the spiritual realm. The early church was blessed with outstanding leaders, especially Paul. He kept the purpose of Christianity constantly before his people. In Galatians 3, he says with much anguish, *"O foolish Galatians, who has bewitched you that you should not obey the truth,* (i.e., fail to grow)?" In 2 Thessalonians 1:3, he commends them, *"We thank God always for you because your faith grows exceedingly."*

What is the goal that God has set before us? -- *"That you will be strengthened with might by His Spirit in the inner man, that Christ may dwell in your hearts by faith, that you being rooted and grounded in love, may be able to comprehend with all the saints what is the breadth and length and depth and height, and to know the love of Christ, which passes knowledge, that you might be filled with all the fullness of God."* (Ephesians 3:16-19)

## Hardship

A poet once said, "I, being woman (or human), am hard beset (everything is against me). I live by squeezing from a stone, the little nourishment I get." These are the words of someone who has tried, and tried, and failed, and feels like giving up. This is often true of Christians. Paul said once, *"O wretched man that I am. Who shall deliver me from this body of death?"* The Romans punished a murderer by tying the victim's body on his back. That's how bad Paul felt.

Another poet wrote these words, "I've tried in vain, a thousand ways my hopes to raise, my fears to quell, but I have found the Bible says, my only hope is Jesus." David failed God and wrote, *"Renew a right spirit within me. A broken and a contrite heart thou wilt not despise.*" Like David, when we see we are not up to the task given us, we should confess our failure and ask for help. The Bible says, "*It is God that works in us, both to will and to do His good pleasure.*" (Philippians 2:13) God puts the desire in us to do His will, and then He enables us to do it.

Hebrews 3:17 tells of Israel failing to enter the Promised Land and how they had to remain in the wilderness for 40 years. God was very upset with them. Then in Chapter 4:1, He tells us we'd better not fail like they did. They failed because they didn't think God would help them. Believing God will help us is called rest. It is standing on His promises. Chapter 4:11 says, "*Let us labor to enter His rest, lest we do the same as Israel did and suffer the consequences.*"

There is only one solution to the hardships of life, and that is to trust God to see you through. Always remember He saved us without any help from us; and in the same way, He can keep us without any help. When Israel decided to obey God and take Jericho, they did nothing but march around the city. It was God who made the walls fall flat. In the same way, God will help those who trust Him.

## Head Knowledge

One of the most successful strategies of Satan in destroying the work of God is to delude people into thinking head knowledge is all that is required. Such knowledge is useful as a preliminary step toward God, but God requires heart knowledge. If a person stops seeking God when he gains a little head knowledge, he is as lost as the one with no knowledge. Some historians know famous people like Lincoln and Washington better than they know themselves but it's just head knowledge. It will never equal heart knowledge. God isn't interested in head knowledge. He's interested in personal friendship.

The Bible is full of examples of the difference between head and heart knowledge. Peter and Judas both learned a lot in following Jesus for three years. They both failed miserably, but they ended up differently. Judas, the treasurer for the disciples, never got beyond head knowledge. When he saw the tide turning against Jesus and his chance of getting easy money slipping away, he betrayed Jesus for 30 pieces of silver.

Peter also saw the tide turning, but he followed Jesus to the courtyard and was heartbroken to see what was happening to Jesus. Then when the servant confronted him about being a disciple of Jesus, he failed, out of fear, and denied his Lord, but when Jesus looked at him, he went out and wept bitterly. He had heart knowledge. Judas ended his life. Peter repented. One was lost; one was saved.

Saul, in the Old Testament, seemed like he'd be a fine king, but when he disobeyed God and Samuel charged him with disobedience, he stonewalled and made excuses. He told Samuel he just wanted to make sacrifices to God. But Samuel said, *"Obedience is better than sacrifice."* He lost the kingship. God said, *"The Lord has sought him a man after His own heart."* The man who replaced him was David, who wrote so many Psalms, sharing his heart with thousands of generations. Jesus said, *"Blessed are the pure in heart, they shall see God."* (Matthew 5:8) *"Man looks on the outward appearance, but God looks on the heart."* (1 Samuel 16:7) *"The eyes of the Lord run to and fro throughout the whole earth, to show Himself strong in the behalf of them whose heart is perfect toward Him."* (2 Chronicles 16:9)

## Hide and Seek

Probably every preschool child in the world played hide and seek. It offers the two things that get people going all through life: a challenge and a reward. Who can forget the fun of finding someone in a very good hiding place!

Believe it or not, this game started in the Garden of Eden. Adam and Eve enjoyed God's company every day, but when they sinned against Him, they thought it was best to hide. God found them, of course, and that was the end of their friendship.

From then on, God dealt with Adam and Eve and his progenies, out of sight. He did show Himself a few times. He appeared to Abraham as three men. (Genesis 18:2) He appeared to Jacob as a man and wrestled with him. (Genesis 32:24) He spoke to Moses face to face. (Exodus 33:11) Apparently, this wasn't enough for Moses, because in verse 18 he asks God to show him His glory. God answered, "*You may not see me and live, but I will put you in a cleft of the rock and cover you with my hand while I pass by. Then I will remove my hand and you will see my back, but not my face.*" A few years later, Moses passed the leadership position to Joshua. Israel was preparing to attack Jericho, when suddenly, a man appeared with his sword in his hand. Joshua asked him if he was a friend or foe. The man replied, "*I come as Chief of the Lord's armies.*" (Joshua 5:14) It doesn't tell us more, but that was God, Himself, in the form of a man, taking charge of the Battle of Jericho.

Centuries passed and Israel became a powerful nation with David as their King. David was so close to God that he was inspired to write most of the Psalms. But even with that advantage, he fell into sin. When he realized what he had done, he pleaded for mercy. The first thing he said was, "*God, don't hide yourself from me.* (Psalm 55:1) "*Don't take your Holy Spirit from me.*" (Psalm 51:11) We don't know if David ever saw God, but spiritually, he walked with Him every day, and God called him a man after His own heart.

Isaiah was right in the middle of a prophecy of the future glory of Israel, when he exclaimed, "*Verily thou art a God that hides thyself.*" (Isaiah 45:15) It sounds like he was a little exasperated.

The period of time in which God deals with man incognito seems to be a test to see who will obey God's voice. "*My sheep hear my voice.*" (John 10:27) "*The just shall live by faith.*" (Romans 1:17) "*Without faith, it is impossible to please God.*" (Hebrews 11:6) God could have shown Himself all along, but His relationship to people would have been based on fear. In fact, the children of Israel were so frightened that they didn't even want to hear His voice. (Exodus 20:19)

God says in Jeremiah 29:13, *"You shall seek me and find me when you search for me with all your heart." "God is a rewarder of them that diligently seek Him."* (Hebrews 11:6) *"Draw near to God and He will draw near to you."* (James 4:8) *"Because of their sin, I hid from them."* (Ezekiel 39:23) *"Today we see through a glass darkly, but then, (when He comes), we will see face to face."* (1 Corinthians 13:12) *"When He shall appear, we shall be like Him, for we shall see Him as He is."* (1 John 3:2)

I believe God's purpose in all this is character building. He is choosing people who will follow Him regardless of difficulties. Remember how He dealt with Job, just to prove that there are people of integrity. Job ended up saying, *"Though He slay me, yet will I trust Him."* There is no other way.

*"The mystery which has been hidden from the beginning - that to the principalities and powers in heavenly places, might be shown, by God's people, the manifold wisdom of God."* (Ephesians 3:10) In other words, God is going to showcase all the people who trust Him in spite of all that Satan hurls at them.

*"Whom having not seen, you love; in whom, though now you see Him, not yet believing, you rejoice with joy unspeakable and full of glory!"* (1 Peter 1:8)

## Holiness

I remember, as a boy, knowing some people that belonged to a holiness church. They were really strict, so I kept hoping my mother would never start going there. I held to that idea for many years, but I finally learned that holiness was the one thing in the whole world that I needed most.

Holiness basically means pure and clean. Who in their right mind would rather be impure and dirty? Today we hear much about pollution, contamination, corruption, etc. Laws are passed to keep the air, soil, and rivers clean, and to root out corruption in business and government. In other words, clean is in and pollution is out. But strange as it may seem, this concept never carries over to spiritual matters. Most Christians think a little bit of sin is okay, since 'nobody can be perfect'. Little do they know how dangerous that idea is. What will they say when they come across Hebrews 12:14, *"Without holiness, no man shall see the Lord."*

Another important word in the Bible is sanctification, which means the same as holiness. Leviticus 20:7 says, *"Sanctify yourselves and be holy."* Verse 26 says, *"You shall be holy to me for I am holy."* The word saint also means holy. Romans 1:7 says, *"All - are called to be saints."* 1 Thessalonians 3:13 says, *"That you may be unblameable in holiness - at the coming of Jesus with all His saints."* Ephesians 5:25-26 says, *"Jesus gave Himself for the church that He might sanctify and cleanse it - and present it to Himself - not having spot or wrinkle."*

Holiness churches teach what they call a second work of grace. First, there is salvation. Then comes sanctification. Salvation is the forgiveness of your past sins. Sanctification is the process of setting you free from the power of sin, i.e., making sure you are holy (pure). Salvation is a free gift. You can't do anything to earn it. Sanctification takes work, not that God doesn't do it for us through the Holy Spirit, but without determination to pursue God, it goes nowhere.

Jesus said, *"If any man will come after me,* (be my disciple, be a learner, one who wants to grow, who wants to become mature, to be holy), *let him deny self, take up his cross, and follow me."* (Matthew 16:24) This is the tight gate and narrow way that only a few people find. (Matthew 7:14) Let him build his life with gold, silver, and precious stones, not with wood, hay, and stubble. (1 Corinthians 3:12) Sanctification is moving from the gospels, which contain the story of Jesus coming into the world, to the epistles of Paul, which include the story of the work of the Holy Spirit in our lives. God didn't save us, as many think in order to populate heaven. He could turn stones into people. His purpose was to have a family of people that are in His image, likeness, and nature. People that are as pure as He is and as loving as He is. In short, people who could live together in peace and harmony.

David is a good example of someone who was determined to stay holy. When he was convicted of his sin (2 Samuel 12:13), he didn't lose any time in confessing it. He said, *My sin is ever before me. When I kept silent, my bones were roaring about all the day long. Your hand was heavy upon me. Cast me not away from your presence. Restore unto me the joy of your salvation.*" (Psalm 32 & 51) This is true repentance, without which there is no forgiveness.

## How Do You Know You're Right?

I get that skeptical look just about every time I talk to someone about becoming a Christian. There's a lot more unbelief out there than belief, and they call this a Christian country! Most people won't give me the time to tell them why I'm sure, so this is the next best thing. Hopefully, they'll find a spare minute to check it out. For the following reasons, I know I am right: I've been studying the Bible (not just reading it) for about 70 years. I've never come across one sentence that raised red flags in my mind; no contradictions, no stretching the truth, no approval of immoral conduct (like offering harems). Instead, the Bible hammers home the truth from beginning to end that righteousness is the only acceptable way to live, that love is the only acceptable way to relate to people, and that there will be a payday where everyone will have to give account. That, to me, proves a mighty God is in charge and is running a tight ship.

The Bible does not present a philosophy, a course in ethics, or an all-powerful force; but rather a personal God, in all points like us, except for sin. The fact of sin is the number one concern of the Bible. Everything that's wrong with the world is due to sin. It is a rebellion, a failure, a rejection of everything that is right and good. The addiction to sin is like having a monkey on your back. You know it's bad and want to get rid of it but can't. The Bible has the only reasonable solution. In an orderly universe, law-breakers must be punished. A house divided cannot stand. On the other hand, God was not willing to destroy His creation. He devised a plan. He would send His Son, the Lord Jesus, to take our sins upon Himself and take our punishment, thus giving us a clean slate. This unbelievable plan was carried out and millions, maybe billions, of people will testify that it works. Just to know that Jesus died to free them from sin turns people into totally new creatures.

The Bible is full of prophecies. If two or three prophecies came true, it would be a powerful argument that the prophecy is of God. If all the prophecies came true, then without doubt they are of God. The most striking, hard to believe prophecy was that Israel would be scattered all over the world for centuries, and then in the last days, be gathered back to their homeland. This happened in 1948 when Israel became a nation again. Also, Jerusalem was prophesied to be trodden down (controlled) by the Gentiles until the age of the Gentiles was over. (Luke 21:24) In the 1967 war, the Jews reconquered Jerusalem. This was the most unlikely event that had ever happened. Along this same line, Jesus said, *"When you see the fig tree budding, you know the end is near."* (Luke 21:29) The tree is a type found in Israel. They have been budding for 50 years. Just think, a people were scattered all over the world, maintained their identity, were gathered back to their homeland, and became prosperous again. Only God could predict something like that.

The Bible offers us a personal relationship with our Creator. Although God is invisible, a relationship can be established by reading His Word. Jesus said, *"Man does not live by bread alone, but by every*

*Word of God."* (Matthew 4:4) David, who was very close to God, said in his 23rd Psalm, *"He makes me lie down in green pastures."* David is comparing himself to a sheep, and just as a sheep enjoys good pasture, so David enjoyed the Word of God. Every true Christian will testify to the nourishment available in the Word of God.

The number one benefit of becoming a Christian is having your sins washed away. The number two benefit is the power to stay clean. John the Baptist introduced Jesus by saying, "He will baptize you in His Holy Spirit, so you can stay clean." Baptism means immersion, being completely submerged. We understand it in connection with water but being submerged in the Holy Spirit has eluded most people. Nevertheless, the experience is there, free for the asking, making the salvation of our souls complete.

For my skeptical friends, this is just the short list of the reasons why I know I'm right. As the Bible says, *"There is no other name under heaven given among men whereby we must be saved."* (Acts 4:12)

## Imagination

Imagination is the act of forming a mental image of something you admire or want. It is a gift from God that helps us in many ways. A young person must imagine what he wants out of life as a means to attain the goal. Later on, he must, in his various pursuits, imagine where they will lead him. Will they advance him or retard him in his life goals? Of course, we all know imagination is one of Satan's favorite tools to trip us. (Genesis 6:5 and Psalm 1:1) It is time for us to turn the tables on him.

Spiritually, imagination is essential. Paul said in Hebrews 11:1, *"Faith is the substance of things unseen, the evidence of things hoped for."* We can substitute the word imagine for faith. Get the image of the thing you hope for, believe it's coming, and keep it before you until it comes to pass. I play the piano for a singing group. When I play a solo,

I've learned that I need to imagine success. Every time I have doubts and fears, I mess up.

It is required of us to be soul winners. It isn't easy, but God makes it happen when we keep the picture of success before us. Abraham was told to sacrifice his son, Isaac. His mind was probably working overtime, trying to see any good coming out of it. He obeyed, because he forced his imagination to see good results coming from the worst circumstances. This pleases God. Joseph had the same experience. His imagination focused on what the Lord showed him in a dream, that he would be a ruler someday. His imagination kept the dream alive through the worst circumstances. David, in his last prayer for his people, remarked about all the blessings God had showered on them and said, "*Lord, keep this forever in the imagination of the thoughts of the hearts of your people.*" (1 Chronicles 29:18) Jesus knew what was in store for Him in this world, but He said, "*I have set my face like a flint and I know I will not be ashamed.*" (Isaiah 50:7) I think that means He imagined the success of His mission every minute of the day and kept negative thoughts out. Hebrews 12:2 says, "*For the joy that was set before Him* (imagination) *He endured the cross.*"

Imagination could be the difference between true worship and false worship. A person who goes through the litanies and liturgies of the church and imagines nothing, but instead lets his mind wander all over, is worshipping in vain. The person who imagines himself being pulled out of a horrible pit (Psalm 40:2), who sees himself being nailed to the cross, which was his due, that person is worshipping in spirit and truth.

Matthew, Mark, Luke, and John had their minds filled with images of all that Jesus said and did. They recorded them in four of the most beautiful books of the Bible. John said there were so many that the world couldn't contain the books that should be written. One of the best things we can do for our spiritual life is to imagine what Jesus would do in our circumstances. We say faith is the victory. That means we see the thing we desire as accomplished and we give Him thanks beforehand. This is the real victory. (Hebrews 13:15) At my advanced age, I'm imagining my reception at the Pearly Gates. I imagine a glorious embrace and the words, *"Well done good and faithful servant. Enter into the joy of the Lord."* I stand on the promise, *"Ask and you shall receive."*

# In Other Words

This article is about Bible translations. 'In other words' is an expression most of us appreciate, because we hope it will give us a better understanding of what has been said. Words are strange creatures. They are not at all like math, where a number has an exact meaning and stays the same. Words are more like a moving target with several rings. To hit the bull's eye, you have to be pretty good. In writing articles, I'm often stymied to find the right word. I use the dictionary and the thesaurus to no avail, and finally have to settle for a word that is second or third best.

It is for this reason that there are so many translations of the Bible. Some people foolishly say the King James is the only version for them. This is a mistake. Some denominations put out their own version and practically condemn all others. This is worse than a mistake. Common sense says no one version is perfect. Look at other versions. Others may come closer to the real meaning or give a different insight. In saying a word is like a moving target, think of all the words that have been used to say someone is special. Long ago, there were hot cats, today they are cool cats. In between, they were keen, swell, sharp, hip, pip, and hunk.

It's the same with Bible words. In King James time, concupiscence was a word. (Colossians 3:5) You'll never hear it today. They'd say, "Lord, keep my soul" (Psalm 25:20), which to us means retain, but to them meant guard. They'd say, "Keep the commandments," which really meant to obey them. Psalm 34:9 says, "O fear the Lord, ye His saints." Fear could be translated to respect, acknowledgement, honor, notice, appreciation, being aware, watching Him, involving Him, revering Him, considering Him, deferring to Him, seeking Him, or knowing that He is there. This should give you a little idea of the problem with words.

In my opinion, one of the best Bibles is the Amplified Bible. As the word suggests, this Bible gives as many meanings to a verse as possible, and some of them are very instructive. For example, Luke 2:13 in the King James Version reads, "*There was with the angel a multitude of the heavenly host.*" The Amplified version says, "*There appeared with the angel an army of the troops of heaven, a heavenly knighthood.*" That's a huge difference.

In 2 Corinthians 1:21-22, the King James version, says, "*He which stablishes us with you in Christ and hath anointed us is God, who hath also sealed us and given the earnest of the Spirit in our hearts.*" The Amplified says, "*God has consecrated and anointed us, enduing us with the gifts of the Holy Spirit, putting His seal upon us and giving us His Holy Spirit in our hearts as the security deposit and guarantee of the fulfillment of His promise.*" There's a lot more to meditate on here than in the King James version.

Ephesians 1:13-14 in the Amplified version says, "*You were stamped with the seal of that long promised Holy Spirit. That Spirit is the guarantee of our inheritance, the first fruit, the pledge, and foretaste, the down payment on our heritage in anticipation of its full redemption and our acquiring complete possession of it.*" Compare that to the King James and I'm sure you'll agree that to say something 'in other words' is a blessing.

## In Person

'In person' means you actually meet the person face to face. The most important question a 'Christian' can ask is this: Do I know the Lord in person or just about Him? Variations of this question would be: Does joining a church mean I know the Lord? Does reading the Bible a lot mean I know the Lord? Does following the golden rule mean I know the Lord? Does being kind and loving mean I know the Lord? Does becoming a pastor or missionary mean I know the Lord? The answer to these questions is no. All these things are good and helpful, but they don't add up to knowing the Lord. They follow knowing the Lord. The first thing a person must do is get right with the Lord Jesus. As long as you're in Satan's family, you're an enemy of God, and as such, nothing you do can be accepted by God. You first must repent of your sins, ask His forgiveness, and receive Jesus in your heart as your Savior. You are then born again into God's family. It's like a man that beats up his wife and then offers to do the dishes. First be reconciled, and then do the good deeds that are acceptable to God. This is putting the cart where it belongs. Putting the cart before the horse will never work.

Most people make light of sin, but it is the worst kind of treason against a loving creator. It started with Adam, who thumbed his nose at God and ate of the forbidden tree. He soon found out how bad his mistake was, but he never apologized. He accepted the curse on the earth, and the curse of death on himself, and passed it on to his children. We, as descendants of Adam, are born with that same treasonous nature, but God, in His tremendous love for us, offers us a pardon for all our sins. However, we must accept it. It is not automatic. It is also not just brushing our sins under the rug. Jesus paid for our pardon by taking our sin and our death sentence. Such love should lead us to repentance, or godly sorrow for our sins, which gives us acceptance with God and the removal of the curse. This transaction leads to the good life.

People need to know that Jesus is knocking at their heart's door (Revelation 3:20), that He wants to sup with them (get acquainted), but they say, "Duh," and go on reading more facts. There needs to be a preacher that will shout from the rooftop, "He wants to talk to you, man." Go back to that verse and say, "Lord, I throw open the door. I'm sorry I didn't catch on. I want to sup with you." What is so hard about that? That's a start. Then, if you can fit a time slot in your busy schedule to meet with Him (the Lord of the universe), and get a conversation going, you will soon find that He's more real than even your family members. Look at what Paul says, *"Everything is worthless compared to the priceless gain of knowing Christ. O, that I might know Him."* (Philippians 3:8-10) *"I pray that Christ will be more and more at home in your hearts, living within you."* (Ephesians 3:17,19) The early church in Acts 2:1 was completely taken up with God. Nothing else mattered. They had met God in person. If you are truly saved, your life will make a 180 degree turn around. You will be more and more occupied with Christ, and more and more attached to him every day, until you can say with Paul, *"I am crucified with Christ, nevertheless I live, yet not I, but Christ lives in me."* (Galatians 2:20) In other words, if you are truly saved, you just won't have any doubts about it.

## Intelligent Design

Several years ago, in a town in Pennsylvania, several Christians on the school board decided to require the teaching of intelligent design to be included with the teaching of evolution. There was a trial, they lost, and were railroaded right off the board.

Anyone taking a thoughtful look at our situation on earth would have to conclude that the only reasonable, logical explanation for our origin and placement on a perfect planet would be the creation story of the Bible. When NASA sends a spacecraft to Mars, the main thing they hope to find is the right air, the right water, the right gravity, and the right plants. Without these items, life would be impossible. Our planet has them all. Air is oxygen, nitrogen, and carbon dioxide in exact proportions. Water is two parts hydrogen and one-part oxygen. Any deviation would be a disaster. How could such exact formulations occur by accident? Night and day are taken for granted, but any other arrangement would be a disaster. The law of seeds producing after their kind is taken for granted, but remove it, and there would be chaos. The laws of sowing and reaping, of recycling, of conservation, of air currents, gulf streams, etc., are all essential to life. The temperature also has to be within a very narrow range for comfort. A little hotter or colder than it is, and we couldn't survive. That means the sun has to be exactly 93 million miles away. The amount of gravity is exactly the right amount to hold us to the earth, and yet allow us to move around. Think of 93 million miles being exactly right for both gravity and heat. How many times do we get something right for one thing, but then it's wrong for something else?

Food supply is absolutely necessary, so there must be plants, animals, and fish. The plants must be the right kind. The good plants contain all the vitamins, etc., we require. Weeds and briers wouldn't do any good. To grow, the good plants must have soil. The soil must have the right nutrients in it. Plants must have energy, must know how to get it from the sun, and must have the right amount of light from the sun. Too much or too little and the plants are dead. The plants must have water brought to them. There's no way the plants can go to the water. This means there must be rain and there must be wind to move the clouds. To have the rain, there must be a water cycle by which the water is drawn up into clouds. To have a water cycle there must be a large mass of water like an ocean. The sun's heat has to be just the right temperature to evaporate the water. There must be cold air in the right place to make the water vapor condense as rain. Besides food plants, there must also be plants for clothing. Animals are just as important for food and clothing, and what would we do without seafood? Flowers, birds, and many animals are important for our enjoyment and happiness. Herbs, spices, etc., are important for flavoring. Other necessities for a livable world would be trees, clay, etc., for building materials; coal, oil, and gas for energy; and iron ore, etc., for industries. Fire is taken for granted, but without the atmosphere there could be no fire. Seasons are taken for granted, but without the tilt of the earth, there would be no seasons. The more you look at the wonders of the earth, the more you know that only an all-powerful God could produce such perfection.

So far, we've only looked at the environment. To look at the human species is a whole new ball game. The design and precision of the body is mind boggling, but then there is the soul, the mind, the personality, the emotions, the will, the imagination, the morals, the conscience, etc., etc., too much for this article, except to say with the Psalmist, "*The fool says there is no God.*"

As we said in the beginning, our education systems believe that all this, as described above, got started with an accidental big bang. Think of it, a library of a million books is an accident, a symphony orchestra is an accident, a family (mother, father, and children) is an accident, a beautiful garden is an accident. A course in probability ordinarily would shoot this idea full of holes on the first day, but for some strange reason, the probability professors never say a mumbling word. I read somewhere about all the parts it takes to make a car, every part precision engineered. Try to imagine anyone saying, "Oh, look what a big bang just produced." The world and its people are a trillion times more precision engineered, and yet all the professors say, "Oh, look what a big bang produced." Actually, a big bang couldn't even produce a cup and saucer.

To make their theory even more bizarre, every part of the earth as described had to be in perfect working order when man appeared on the scene. Otherwise, he couldn't survive. The acceptance of this theory has to rank right up there with the Seven Wonders of the World. The toleration of it by intelligent people, especially Christians, is another wonder. Paul said the wrath of God is hanging over people that push away the truth, for from the time the world was created, people have seen the earth, and sky, and all that God made. They can see His power and divine nature. They have no excuse. "*Professing themselves to be wise, they became fools --- they worshipped the things God made, but not the creator.*" (Romans 1:18-25) Paul saw it in his day, but my guess is it's worse today than ever.

# Is This All There Is?

A man buys a hundred acres of land, clears the brush and trees, plows the ground, plants crops, a vineyard, fruit trees, and flowers. Everything grows. He builds barns, silos, a house, a workshop, etc. Soon he has a prosperous farm, the envy of all, and then when everything is perfect, he has a heart attack, dies, and is put in a hole in the ground.

Another man does well in school and decides to work his way through college. He achieves great success and decides to keep working for a PhD degree. He finally finishes his education and takes a job with a prestigious company. He begins the climb up the corporate ladder and, after many years, becomes the president. By now, he has a beautiful home, several cars, etc., but he has a heart attack and dies, and is put in a hole in the ground.

Isn't there something wrong with these stories? The question naturally pops up, "Why would anybody do all that sacrificing and work, since it's for nothing?" Some will say, "It's for the children," but obviously, they're in the same boat. They, too, will work hard for a lifetime and then be put in a hole in the ground. Yes, it is for nothing.

Jesus said if you gain the whole world, what good is it in the end? I was at an auction and saw a large table piled up with picture frames. There were college degrees and distinguished service awards, etc., in the frames. They sold for a dollar or two apiece. This calls for some serious reflection.

Most people accept this as normal. This is the way it's supposed to be. They never wonder if something might be wrong. It doesn't bother them that life seems pointless. They don't search for answers. All they know is to eat, drink, and be merry, while you can.

There is an answer in the Bible. This weary round of working for nothing is not the original plan. It is plan B. The original plan was for people to live forever, to enjoy the fruits of their labor forever. Our first parents ran afoul of the law and brought the judgment of a short lifespan, hard labor, and death upon us all. But this short life is God's mercy to us. It is long enough to prove that we want to be restored to His favor, that we will obey Him.

Those who ignore this second chance and choose the short-term pleasures of this world will find they have a lot more to worry about than being put in a hole in the ground. God paid a huge price to provide a second chance. He gave His Son to take the punishment of our sins - clear our names. If we ignore this, we must take the punishment ourselves. The Bible says, *"It is a fearful thing to fall into the hands of the living God."* It also says, *"The Lord will bring judgment on those who refuse to accept His plan to save them through the Lord Jesus Christ."* (Hebrews 10:31) *"They will be punished in everlasting hell, forever separated from the Lord."* (2 Thessalonians 1:8) *"What makes us think that we can escape if we are indifferent to the great salvation announced by the Lord Jesus Himself."* (Hebrews 2:3) *"The same shall drink of the wine of the wrath of God, which is poured out without mixture."* (Revelation 14:10)

The other side of the coin says, *"Come, let us talk this over. No matter how deep the stain of your sins, I can take it out and make you clean as snow. If you be willing and obedient, you shall eat the good of the land."* (Isaiah 1:18)

## Israel

One of the most interesting stories in the Bible centers around how Israel became a nation. It began with Abraham, who had a son, Isaac, who had two sons, Esau and Jacob. The name Jacob means deceiver, and the name fitted his character until he was converted. From then on, his name was Israel, meaning a prince or son of God. Israel had twelve sons, each one becoming the head of a tribe.

Joseph was a pivotal son. He had a dream of becoming great and his family bowing down to him. His brothers were furious at the idea that they would bow down to their youngest brother, but it turned out that he was right. In due time, he became the Prime Minister of Egypt and they did bow down to him. While he was in this position, there was a famine in the land that affected Joseph's family, so Joseph invited them to live in Egypt where they had stored up plenty of food. Little did Joseph know that they would stay there 400 years, grow to two million souls and become slaves. The Bible says they had to serve with rigor and hard bondage. They cried to God for help and He heard them.

He remembered His covenant with Abraham, Isaac, and Jacob and determined to set them free. He called Moses to be his spokesman and sent him to Pharaoh to demand their release. Of course, Pharaoh refused, so God arranged many plagues to afflict the land. The last one was the worst. Every Egyptian family's firstborn son would die. After their sons died, Pharaoh decided to let Israel go. Imagine two or three million people leaving their homes and marching into a wilderness. Imagine being the leader of such a mob. As can be expected, the ex-slaves had plenty of problems even with God helping them. Actually, their main problem was in trusting God to help them. Whenever they ran out of water or food, they blamed God for their troubles and wished they could go back to Egypt. This was in spite of seeing God's miracles, especially taking them across the Red Sea on dry ground. It never seemed to register that God would take care of them. They finally reached the Promised Land but became completely demoralized at the thought of fighting for it. God told them to wander in the wilderness for forty years before trying again.

On the second try, they had a new leader named Joshua (the same name as Jesus). Under his leadership, they conquered the land and became a powerful nation. Their greatest leader was King David, who was not only the ruler, but also the spiritual leader that kept them from straying away from God. After David, it was all downhill. Solomon, his son, was unfaithful to God, and following him, there were more wicked kings than good. Israel was finally destroyed seventy years after they rejected Jesus, their Messiah.

What lesson can we learn from their history? The Bible says everything that happened to them is an example for us, *"to the intent that we should not lust after evil things as they did, or be idolaters, and fornicators, or complainers. Now all these things happened to them for our examples and are written for our admonition."* (1 Corinthians 10:6 & 11) In other words, the whole story is an object lesson, designed to keep us from going astray and being destroyed.

# Justice

Justice, or fairness, is something everyone wants. Children are always crying out, "That isn't fair." So, it's a trait we're probably born with, and understandably so, since the world is made up of sinners. Crimes, arguments, complaints, and disputes are universal. There just has to be a system for resolving them. You can believe the justice department of any country is a very big operation. It's interesting to note that for every dispute that goes to court, one side will lose. For a million cases, 500,000 people will say, "There's no justice!" Fortunately for us, God is the author of justice. A large part of His Word is devoted to the problem of settling disputes.

The first court case in history was the crime of the ages, committed by our first parents. They defied a very strict law of God. *"If you disobey and eat of the forbidden tree, you will die."* (Genesis 2:17) Justice demanded that the death sentence be carried out. If God had brushed their crime under the rug, the world would be lawless and chaotic. On the other hand, God loved the man He created and was not willing to let him perish, so what could He do? Even the mighty God could not break the law! There were only two ways that the problem could be solved. One was to destroy His creation. The other was to destroy Himself. What a choice! What a dilemma! Who ever heard of somebody offering himself to be destroyed to save somebody else?

God gave a preview of this terrible predicament when He asked Abraham to sacrifice his son. (Genesis 22) Abraham was spared from actually doing it; but, *"God spared not His own Son, but delivered Him up for us all."* (Romans 8:32) In Hebrews 10:5-14, Jesus spoke before creation saying, *"A body hast thou prepared for me - I come to do Thy will - to be sacrificed for sins - by which mankind can be sanctified - made perfect forever."* These verses are possibly the most profound in the Bible. Jesus was the Lamb, slain from the foundation of the earth. (Revelation 13:8) Before creation, God knew man would sin, and Jesus, the second person of the trinity, volunteered at that time to die in man's place. Did He know what kind of death it would be? God knows everything. He knew, and He still volunteered. As the song says, "The love of God is greater far, than tongue or pen can ever tell. It goes beyond the highest star and reaches to the lowest hell." There's a verse in the Bible that says, *"Mercy and truth are met together. Righteousness and peace have kissed each other."* (Psalm 85:10) Another way to say it is, love and justice kissed each other. Yet another way is, God so loved man that He allowed His only begotten Son to take his death penalty that man should not perish but have everlasting life. God did the unimaginable.

The first thing God did after Adam and Eve sinned was to kill two lambs. (Genesis 3:1) Adam and Eve must have been horrified to see the first killing in the world, but they needed to see the consequences of their sin and to know what they were up against. They were given to understand that those two lambs died in their place. They were to be temporary substitutes for God's Son who would come in due time and pay their penalty. They, of course, didn't understand God's plan in full, but they knew they had been saved from something very horrible.

After many centuries, in the fullness of time, John the Baptist came on the scene and announced, *"Behold the Lamb of God that takes away the sins of the world."* Jesus had finally come. For three years, He taught, exhorted, and, with tears, pleaded that His people would turn from sin (Luke 19:41), but their will to sin was set like concrete. In the

Garden of Gethsemane, Jesus confirmed His willingness to be offered up and immediately the powers of darkness seized Him and set up a mock trial to condemn Him. On the very day of the Passover, when the Jews were fulfilling the offering of the sacrificial lamb, Jesus, the true Lamb, was killed. His last words, "Father, forgive them," prove that justice had been served and man could be forgiven.

Now for the critical part of this settlement. It is not a blanket forgiveness of all people. John 3:16 says, *"For God so loved the world that He gave His only begotten Son that whosoever believeth on Him should not perish, but have everlasting life."* John 1:1 says, *"As many as receive Him, they are saved."* Notice the two key words, believe and receive. Fail to do this and you're as lost as ever. God will not force anyone to believe. That would violate justice, but neither can He annul the death sentence. All who reject this offer will have to pay the penalty themselves. *"The soul that sins must die."* (Ezekiel 18:4 and Romans 6:3) Of all the tragedies of this world, this is the worst, that people ignore, despise, and refuse such a wonderful offer. A man in a mission was convicted of his sin and prayed out loud, "God, I don't want justice. I want mercy." His eyes had been opened.

## Light

"Not with drums, light comes. It is gentle, unobtrusive. It will not open doors or go around corners like sound does, but it will enter every place that is open." These, as I recall, are the first lines of a poem that I enjoyed long ago. However, the thought about light has lingered, especially as to how it relates to God. We read in Romans 1:20, *"The invisible things of God are seen and understood by the things that are made* (things we can see)." First off, we know that God is light, from reading 1 John 1:5 and John 8:12, so it's certain we can learn much from light.

The first characteristic of light is its invisibility. We don't see light. We see the objects that reflect light. God, as a Spirit, is invisible, but He can be seen as reflected in His people. The moon is another example of reflected light.

The second characteristic of light is what has already been alluded to in the poem. Light is gentle, just like God. It doesn't force its way into any place. Light is not like sound, which to me can be torturous at times! In 1 Thessalonians 2:7 & 11, Paul tells how he treated his converts saying, "*We were as gentle with you as a nurse and as a father.*" These words came from a former murderer. This is the change that takes place when one lets the light in. He becomes as gentle as light. Isaiah 42:1-4 said this about Jesus, "*He will not fight nor shout nor crush the weak or quench hope.*" Any opaque surface can stop light. And God, having given man free will, allows him to block out the light, but warns of the consequences.

The third characteristic of light is also alluded to in the poem. Light goes in straight lines. It doesn't turn corners. John the Baptist, the introducer of Jesus, went straight to his task and went straight to the problem. "You snakes," he said to the Pharisees (Matthew 3:7). Jesus also went straight to His task. In Mark 1:10, He was baptized in water and straightway He was baptized in the Spirit; in verse 12, He was straightway driven into the wilderness to be tested; in verse 20, He straightway called the disciples; in verse 21, He straightway went into the Synagogue and taught; in verse 28, His fame immediately spread abroad; in verse 31, He immediately healed the sick. In Luke 4:28-29, they mobbed Him and tried to kill Him, and in verse 30, He walked straight through them!

The fourth characteristic is its mystery. Believe it or not, no one knows what light is. There are theories, but no agreement. It is shrouded in mystery. How fitting a picture of God. Isaiah 45:15 says, "*God hides Himself.*" For thousands of years, people have looked for God in all the wrong places and, of course, they can't agree on who or what God is. God does proclaim Himself to be mysterious. 1 Corinthians 2:7 says, "*We speak the wisdom of God in a mystery.*" Romans 11:33 says, "*His ways are past finding out.*" 1 Timothy 3:16

says, *"Great is the mystery of Godliness."* Isaiah 55:9 says, *"As the heaven are higher than the earth, so are my thoughts than yours."* To those who can't find time for God, He will always be a mystery, but to those who seek Him, He may be found. (Isaiah 55) Where do you seek Him? In the Bible. God's Word is Spirit and light. (John 6:63)

The fifth characteristic of light is that it is our only source of life. The magic word is photosynthesis. It means put together with light! Without it, we wouldn't have anything to eat. It happens in plants. We should acknowledge this miracle every day, at least when we sit down to eat! Likewise, the only source of eternal life is Jesus. The miracle of the incarnation and substitutionary atonement alone gives us salvation. John 1:4 says, *"In Him (Jesus) was life and the life was the light of men."* We can turn this around and say in Him was light and the light was the life of men. The light, the life, and the Word are all the same. Psalm 119:5 says, *"Thy Word is a lamp and a light."* Psalm 119:10 says, *"The entrance of Your Word gives light."* Matthew 4:1 says, *"People that sat in the dark saw the light."* That is, they heard the Word of God. They saw the righteousness and holiness of God, compared to the darkness, evil, impurity, and wickedness of Satan. If they accepted the truth, they became children of light. (1 Thessalonians 5:5) In this physical world, we can't live without sunlight. In the spiritual world, we can't live without "Son" light.

The sixth characteristic of light is that it is our only source of water, which makes it as important as photosynthesis. The magic words are evaporation and condensation. The sun draws up the water from the earth and returns it as the gentle rain. Question: How many thank the Lord for a rainy day? The Lord uses showers as an illustration of the moving of His Spirit. *"My speech shall distill as showers on the grass."* (Deuteronomy 32:2) *"There shall be showers of blessing."* (Ezekiel 4: 6) *"Ask the Lord for rain --- He shall give showers of rain."* (Zechariah 10:1) *"As the rain comes down - so shall my Word be."* (Isaiah 55:10) *"He will give you the former rain and the latter rain. I will pour out my Spirit."* (Joel 2:23 & 28) *He will rain righteousness on you "* (Hosea 10:12). Pray much for rain.

The seventh characteristic of light is a very personal one. Light enables us to see. Where would we be without sight? How would we know where we were going? Everyone agrees that physical sight is absolutely necessary. But how many agree that to know about Jesus and heaven, and Satan and hell, and how to make the transfer from one to the other, is even more important? Jesus said it would be much better to be blind physically than to be blind spiritually. (Mark 9:47) Of the Christian He says, "*You were darkness, now you are light* " (Ephesians 5:8) Paul said he never stopped, "*Praying for his people that the eyes of their understanding be enlightened, they would know the hope of God's calling and the riches of the glory of His inheritance in the saints .*" (Ephesians 1:18)

The eighth characteristic of light is its healing quality. Years ago, it was considered important to get as much sunshine as possible. Today, they're not so sure. But everyone will agree that sunlight has a cheerful, uplifting effect on people. We never welcome an overcast day with, "What a beautiful day!" Malachi 4:2 says, "*Unto you that fear my name shall the sun of righteousness arise with healing in His wings.*" When He comes to the world or to the individual, He will dispel all darkness, and wickedness, and evil, and disease, and pollution that today engulf the world (and individuals).

The ninth characteristic is its spectrum of colors. By passing a light through a prism, the light is divided into a band of colors, from infrared to ultraviolet. God used the prism shape of raindrops to give us the rainbow. We remember Joseph's coat of many colors and the colors used in the tabernacle. All of them are significant.

The tenth characteristic is the speed of light. In an instant, it can go around the world more than seven times at 186,000 miles per second. God is omnipotent, so we must believe that anything He wants to do can be done in an instant, including creating the world. This might stretch your thinking, which is good. There is a reference to Satan flying out of heaven like lightning in Luke 10:18. There's also a reference to our change occurring in a moment, in the twinkling of an eye, in 1 Corinthians 15:52.

The eleventh characteristic of light is a recent development called the laser beam, meaning the amplification of light into a narrow, intense beam, which can burn a hole in a diamond! That sounds pretty frightening. We can only hope it will be used for good purposes. This does tell us that God can do anything with speed and great power. We all know about the flood and should know what's ahead for the world. In 2 Peter 3:10, we read, *"The day of the Lord will come as a thief - in which the heavens shall pass away with a great noise and the elements shall melt with fervent heat."* This is a grim reminder of how dark the world is, and what payday will be like.

To shorten this study, we will bunch up a few more characteristics and challenge you to see the spiritual correlation:

> *Light is usually accompanied by warmth;*
> *Light is free (not like coal, oil, lumber, etc.):*
> *The sun has a tremendous gravitational force, holding the planets in their orbits. Are we in His orbit?*
> *Light is everywhere. The highest-powered telescopes report lights as far as they can see;*
> *Light is a reward.*
> Daniel 12:3 says, *'They that be wise shall shine as the brightness of the firmament and they that turn many to righteousness as the stars forever and ever."*

We conclude with two quotes: Matthew 6:22 says, *"The light of the body is the eye. If the eye be single* (a narrow beam - only having eyes for Jesus), *the body will be full of light,"* and Matthew 5:16 says, *"Let your light so shine before men that they may see your good works and glorify your Father."*

# Make Believe

Would you believe for even a minute, that everything in this world is make believe, and almost everyone is playing a game of make believe? Well, sad to say, heartbreaking really, that's what's happening, and when people die, then reality will hit them. It's hard to blame them, since they're taught from childhood, that what you see is real. Get as much as you can out of it. The one who ends up with the most toys is the most successful, etc. It certainly sounds right and it looks right, but it's wrong. As solid and substantial as a house and a car, etc., look, they're all make believe. There's no real value, no permanence. Even in our limited understanding, we can see that all is change and decay. I lived in one house that burned down, another that was torn down. I'd like to see them again, but they're gone.

The Bible has the final word on the reality of this world. Hebrews 1:11 says, *"Everything will disappear into nothingness; they will become worn out like old clothes folded up and replaced."* Genesis 2:19 says we are dust and we're going back to dust. I never understood these verses until I remembered that everything is made of atoms. An atom is not something solid (something you can see). It is a system of electromagnetic forces. The source of power is God. At any moment that pleases God, this world can be terminated. We read in 2 Peter 3:11, *"Seeing that all these things shall be dissolved, what manner of persons ought ye to be?"* That's the main question we need to face. We should echo the cry of the people in Acts 2:37 after they heard that Jesus died for their sins. *"Men and brethren, what should we do?"*

First, we should get serious about getting answers to the big questions of life. We should be like the Bereans. They got honorable mention in the Bible for looking for answers. (Acts 17:11) If we look hard enough, we will find that there is something real in the world after all.

Next, fix it firmly in your mind that this world is in a transition mode. Don't put all your eggs in this basket. It's heading for the terminal, which means its end. If your dream is to have a bigger and better house, forget it. Paul says, *"We know when our earthly house is dissolved, we have a house, not made with hands, eternal in the heavens* "In 1 Corinthians 3:11, Paul describes the real house we should be concerned about. "Be sure to have the right foundation, which is Jesus Christ." Choose the best material. You can build with gold and silver or sticks and straw. The house you build here and now is the house you will live in forever. What does the gold, silver, sticks, and straw represent? These are spiritual qualities that you develop. Silver and gold represent serving the Lord with all your heart. Sticks and straw represent serving the Lord with a tiny bit of your heart - like five minutes a week. For example, Jesus told of a woman that gave a couple of cents to the Lord's work. A wealthy man gave much more. Jesus said the woman gave the most because it was all she had. The wealthy man gave little in comparison to the amount of his riches. (Mark 12:42) One of them was building with straw. In another case, a man made a long flowery prayer. (Luke 18:11) Jesus said the man did it to impress the people. The man, unknowingly, was building with straw.

In conclusion, the only reality in this world is Spiritual. All else will go to the dustbin of history. Jesus said, *"Heaven and earth shall pass away, but my words shall not."* (Mark 13:31) *"The words I speak are Spirit and life."* (John 6:63) *"A man's life does not consist in the abundance of things."* (Luke 12:15) *"What does it profit if a man gain the whole world and lose his soul?"* (Matthew 16:26) About 85 years ago, I remember playing some kind of make-believe game. It didn't do any harm at that stage, but if I had kept playing it past childhood, I would have been in big trouble. The world today is in big trouble. It's taking a headlong plunge into the abyss. It will not turn around. It's like a ship going down. It's now every man for himself. No one has to go down with the ship. The Bible says, *"Whosoever shall call upon the name of the Lord* (sincerely) *shall be saved."* (Joel 2:32) Some of the saddest words in the Bible are, *"Why will you die?"* (Ezekiel 18:31)

If this applies to you, why not change your situation right now. All you need to do is admit you're a sinner, repent (be sorry for offending God), ask for forgiveness, believe Jesus died for your sins, thank Him for His mercy and begin to tell others what great thing Jesus did for you. The moment you do this, your name is written in God's book of life. (Revelation 20:12)

## Mysteries

The Bible should be marketed as a mystery thriller. It has mysteries that surpass all others. Although others involve life and death, the mysteries of the Bible deal with eternal life and death, and of course, the Bible is truth, not fiction. If there ever was a "must read" book, the Bible is it.

The word mystery means something that is unknown or hard to figure out. Take the parables that Jesus used in His teaching. Even the disciples didn't know what to make of them so they asked Him, "Why do you teach in parables?" Listen to His answer: *"These people have hard hearts. They've closed their eyes and ears to the truth, lest at any time they should be converted."* (Matthew 13:10) In other words, they weren't interested in His teaching, so why bother to explain it to them. In John 7:17, He went further, *"If any man is determined to do God's will* (wants to please God), *he will understand the teaching, the mystery will unfold for him."* There is the key to all Bible mysteries: just get serious!

A classic example of missing the boat is the nation of Israel. All through their history, they were taught that a messiah (savior) was coming and that he would be the sacrificial lamb that would save them from their sins. Take just one prophecy: *"He was wounded for our transgressions - by His stripes we are healed. He was led as a lamb to the slaughter. When you make His soul an offering for your sins, He will see His children."* In other words, you will be saved. (Isaiah 53:5,7&10) That seems plain enough, but they couldn't see it because they just weren't interested. They've been paying for their mistake ever since. I have had first-hand experience of other's lack of interest. I talk to a friend who enjoys my articles about the Lord quite often, and I tell him to read the gospels. He always says, "Yes, yes, I will." But when I ask him how he's doing, he says, "Not yet, I'm too busy." Like Israel, he seems interested, but his actions prove he's not. Like Israel, he will pay for his failure for a long time.

Paul had this to say about mysteries in 1 Corinthians 2:7-14 *"We speak the wisdom of God in mysteries - God hath revealed them to us by His Spirit - that we might know the things that are freely given to us by God. The unsaved man can't understand Bible mysteries because they are Spiritually discerned."* John 14:26 says, *"The Holy Spirit - will teach you all things."* This teaching by the Holy Spirit must be sought. There is no such thing as gaining knowledge or wisdom without work. But what rewards there are for those who study and meditate. Mysteries such as the Incarnation, the Resurrection, the Second Coming, the Trinity, the Baptism in the Holy Spirit, the fulfillment of prophecies, definitely take time and the help of the Holy Spirit. That we are expected to learn about them is seen in the third chapter of 1 Corinthians. Paul says, *"I could not speak to you as to spiritual people for you are still babie*s (spiritually). *I have fed you with milk* (elementary truth), *not with meat* (the mysteries)." Paul was clearly disappointed.

After the resurrection of Christ, two disciples were on their way to Emmaus when a stranger joined them. They told him how disappointed they were that Jesus had been crucified, and how all their hopes were dashed. Then the stranger said, "O fools, and slow of heart to believe the prophets." Then he showed them all the scriptures that told of Jesus coming into the world as a substitutionary lamb. A short time later, the stranger revealed himself to be Jesus, and then He disappeared.

One can't help but realize that if we don't gain understanding of God's mysteries, we are, in God's sight, fools.

# Names of God

There are many names for God, and they all have a special meaning. For example, Jehovah (the eternal one), is combined with Jireh (will provide), Nissi (my banner), Shalom (my peace), and so forth. One name in Exodus 3:15 really caught my attention. First notice what God says to Moses in verse 14, *"I Am that I Am. - Then shalt thou say to the children of Israel, I Am hath sent me to you."* Now verse 15 reads, *"Say unto the children of Israel, the Lord God of your fathers, the God of Abraham, Isaac and Jacob hath sent me to you. This is my name forever and this is my memorial unto all generations."* The last sentence is what grabbed me. This statement practically demands that we find out what it means. We know that names in the Old Testament meant something. This is quite different from today where names mean nothing. If they do mean something, people don't know what it is. What a pity!

Looking up the meaning of these names, we find that Abraham means 'of a great multitude'. Isaac means 'laughter' and Jacob means 'deceiver', not much to go on there. After some meditation on Genesis 12 and following, we see that God planned to make Abraham the father of millions of people, *"as the dust of the earth"* (13:16), and they would bring great blessings to the world. Abraham is the beginner of the Jewish race, which blessed the world with the Bible, the Savior, and ultimately, the millennium. Two other events in Abraham's life should always inspire us: The first was his obedience and faith when he was told to leave his country and, *"Go to a land I will show you."* Hebrews 11:8 says, *"He went out, not knowing where he was going."* The second event was his obedience and faith when he was told to sacrifice his son, Isaac. *"He believed that God was able to raise Isaac up, even from the dead."* (Hebrews 11:19)

The name Isaac means laughter. It seemed to be an unplanned name. When God told Abraham that he would have a son, even though he was 100 years old, Abraham laughed. (Genesis 17:17) Later, the Lord repeated this promise in Sarai's presence, and she laughed. It seems like God wants us to focus on this laughter. We don't find God laughing much in the Bible. In Psalm 2, He laughs at the people that want to do away with Jesus. I'm sure it looked to God like little ants were trying to do away with Him. After God laughs, He says, *"Yet, in spite of your plans to get rid of my Son, He will one day rule the world and He will rule with a rod of iron."* How foolish can people be to think they can obstruct God's plans and run the world their own way? I also see the suggestion that believers can laugh all they want, but no matter how powerful the world seems to be, in the end, they will all bow their heads and say, "Guilty as charged." Then, *"He will execute judgment on all that are ungodly, of their ungodly deeds, which they have ungodly committed and of all their hard speeches which ungodly sinners have spoken against Him."* (Jude 15)

Moving on to the name Jacob, there is the most beautiful story. We have to wonder what happened to cause parents to name their son 'deceiver', which is what Jacob means. Sad to say, Jacob was true to his name. He deceived his father and his brother, Esau. Then he ran away. Years later, the Lord told him to return. He deserves credit for obeying, but when he was almost home, he heard that his brother was coming to meet him with 400 men. He knew this would be the end of him and his whole family. He spent a whole night in prayer and God answered his prayer. He changed Esau, who was planning to kill Jacob, into reconciling with him instead. He also changed Jacob from a deceiver to a prince. From then on, his name was Israel, a prince, or a son of God. It would be well for us when we pray to the Lord as the God of Abraham, Isaac, and Jacob, to recall what the names mean.

Abraham (the father of a multitude) was the father of the Jewish race that God used to bring us salvation; was the man of faith in leaving his homeland and in believing God's promise of a son; and was the man willing to obey God in offering to sacrifice his son.

Isaac (laughter) was the miracle son of Abraham. Abraham and Sarah both laughed when told they would have a son, but the promise came true. Laughter should be part of our worship as we contemplate God's ability to do as He promised

Jacob (deceiver) became a son of God when he got serious enough to spend a night in prayer for help.

*"This is my memorial unto all generations."* (Exodus 3:15)

## Natural – Spiritual

Romans 8:6 says, *"To be naturally minded is death. To be spiritually minded is life and peace."*

It's natural to wake up, see the sunlight, and think, "Oh, what a beautiful morning. Everything's going my way." It's spiritual to say, "Lord, I thank you for waking me up, for giving me another day, for giving me the energy to get up and go to work. Let me walk with you today. Lord, let me not want everything my way, but everything your way."

It's natural to go to breakfast and think, "Oh, just what I like, pancakes and syrup." It's spiritual to say, "Lord, I thank you for this food, but I know I'm going to face some problems today. Lord, feed me with the living bread so I'll be strong to do your will."

It's natural to go to work thinking, "How in the world am I going to face that customer (boss, client, patient, etc.). I'd like to just quit. It's impossible!" It's spiritual to say, "Lord, you said I should lean on you, acknowledge you, wait on you, ask, and receive from you. I'm going to do what you said. Lord, direct my steps, my thoughts and my words."

It's natural to pout, sulk and feel miserable, when everything goes dead wrong. It's spiritual to encourage oneself in the Lord, to say, "Lord, I don't know how you can make this work for good, but you said you could in Romans 8:28. I will stand on that promise. I'm thanking you now for a good day."

It's natural when they tell you that you've got a brain tumor to get severely depressed, to cry out to God, "It isn't fair. I'm too young to die." It's spiritual to say, "Lord, I'm yours. This world is not my home. It's better to be with you than to be here. Lord, I accept your will whether it's to die or to live."

It's natural to almost curse the person that cut you off at an intersection and caused you to have an accident. It's spiritual to say, "Lord, I don't know everything. Maybe he couldn't help it. Maybe I was at fault. Lord, keep me in perfect peace as you promised to those who keep their mind on you." (Isaiah 26:3)

It's natural to get impatient with a son or daughter who's making wrong decisions. They're too old to spank, so you just tell them what you think in very harsh tones. It's spiritual to say something in love and then commit it to the Lord and stand on God's promise, "You will be saved and your house." (Acts 16:31)

It's natural to kick someone who kicked you. It's spiritual to say, "Lord they don't know you. They're under Satan's control. They're going to die and go to hell. Lord, I pray for them to be saved."

It's natural when you mess up a teaching assignment (or any job), to say, "That's it. I'm not cut out for that kind of work. Let them find somebody else." It's spiritual to say, "Lord, I messed up. I'm sorry. If you'll help me, I'll try again. I remember David made some mistakes and he didn't quit."

It's natural when someone takes advantage of you to the tune of thousands of dollars, to keep it in your mind, hoping for a way to retaliate. It's spiritual to forget it, to say, "Lord you gave it to me and you took it away. I will bless the Lord anyway." I believe what you said,

*"Seek first the Kingdom of God and all these things will be added to you."* (Matthew 6:33)

It's natural when someone lies to you to want to say, "Brother, I see you have a problem with telling the truth. Would you like me to give you some pointers?" It's spiritual to say, "Lord, show him the difference between a lie and the truth. Open his eyes to the truth of the gospel."

When you get a bum rap, it's natural to say, "I was framed. I'll get even with them." It's spiritual to say, "Lord, you know my heart. I will wait on you to change this."

One classic example of no retaliation is the story of Joseph. His brothers hated him, planned to kill him, changed their minds, and then sold him as a slave. As a slave, he was falsely charged with attacking a woman and was put in prison. In all of this, he never showed bitterness. Then when God exalted him to be the ruler of Egypt, and his brothers came to him for food, he received them graciously and even excused their wickedness by saying, *"You meant it for evil, but God meant it for good."* He was a spiritual man. Jesus, the Prince of Peace, said as He was dying on the cross, *"Father forgive them, they know not what they do."* Stephen, who was of the same spirit, said the same thing as they stoned him to death.

In all these situations, keep in mind Romans 8:6, *"To be selfish* (fleshly, lower nature, carnal), *leads to deat*h." When you act that way, you are the enemy of God. The law of God, of peace, of life, is to deny yourself, take up your cross, and follow Jesus. (Matthew 16:24) If at any time, we slip from spiritual to natural, we should immediately stop what we're doing, confess our sin, and ask forgiveness. *"If we confess our sins, God is faithful and just to forgive us our sins."* (1 John 1:9)

# One Thing

Did you ever have a boss say to you, "Look man (or woman), one thing you'd better get straight." That's one red flag that gets your attention. It takes priority over everything else. The boss has just emphasized as strongly as possible how he felt about something; how important it was to him. There is a finality in just the sound of those two words, 'one thing'.

David, Jesus, Paul and a blind man used these two words to express their conviction, their certainty that in this world, only one thing matters. Everything else is secondary. They're saying loud and clear: "Don't give your time and energy to anything else." Now, take a little test. Write down what you think the "one thing" is.

David said, *"One thing have I desired of the Lord. That will I seek after, that I may dwell in the house of the Lord all the days of my life, to behold the beauty of the Lord, and to inquire in His temple."* (Psalm 27:4) In other words, the one thing was to know the Lord better, to be with Him, to admire Him, and to converse with Him. Earlier, as a young shepherd, David had written the 23rd Psalm and expressed the same sentiments as to how wonderful the Lord was and how he just wanted to be with Him forever. But now David was a king. He only had to say the word to get anything he wanted. But he had discovered the secret of life: Only one thing matters. Take the whole world but give me Jesus. No turning back, no turning back.

In Luke 10:42, there's the story of Jesus being entertained by sisters, Mary and Martha. Martha was very busy preparing dinner. She saw Mary just sitting and talking to Jesus, so she said to Him, *"Tell her to help me."* Jesus said, *"Martha, Martha, one thing is needful, only one thing is worth being concerned about and Mary has chosen it."* What was it? Just talking and listening to Jesus, the same thing that David wanted.

In Philippians 3:7-13, Paul is giving one of the most eloquent, impassioned utterances of all time. You can almost hear him shouting: *"One thing I do. I am bringing all my energies to bear; I am straining to reach the end of the race; I am pressing toward the mark for the prize of the high calling of God."* What was the prize that Paul was seeking? The very same as David and Mary wanted, to know Jesus in the most intimate way. He said, *"Oh, that I might know Him and the power of His resurrection and the fellowship of His suffering."* (Philippians 3:10)

In John 9, we read the story of the healing of the blind man. The Pharisees were outraged that Jesus did it on the Sabbath, and they told the man that Jesus was a sinner. The man replied I don't know about that, but one thing I do know. I was blind, but now I see! This is the kind of certainty (faith) that the Lord requires for salvation. If you waiver in believing, you will get nothing. (James 1:6 & 7) That one thing makes all the difference.

In Luke 18:18, a rich young ruler came to Jesus and asked Him what he should do to be sure of heaven. Jesus said in verse 22, *"You lack one thing. Sell everything you have and follow me."* The one thing here is about commitment. To be one of God's chosen, you must commit all to Him. You must tell the Lord, *"Everything I have comes from you and I only give you what is yours already."* (1 Chronicles 29:14) If you can't say that, you're lacking the one thing that is required, and will end up losing everything.

Jesus said in His high priestly prayer, *"This is life eternal, that they might know you, the only true God and Jesus Christ whom you have sent."* (John 17:3) There are various levels of knowing the Lord, from slight acquaintance, like the thief on the cross, to Paul's words in Ephesians 3:19, *"That you might know the love of Christ which passes knowledge; that you might be filled with all the fullness of God."* This is the prize of the high calling of God, the one thing we should seek.

If you follow this one thing, *"An entrance shall be ministered unto you abundantly into the everlasting Kingdom of our Lord and Savior, Jesus Christ."* (2 Peter 1:11)

## Patterns

A pattern is a guide to go by when making something. Synonyms would be an example, or a model. When someone wants to make something, anything from a dress to a battleship, he's sure to get a pattern. The Christian who wants to live the kind of life that God wants, likewise needs a pattern, something to go by. It so happens, or I should say, God designed it so, that the Old Testament is full of patterns. Everything that happened back there, in some way, is an example of what we should be doing, or how we should do it. (1 Corinthians 10:6) Hebrews 8:5 says, "See that you go by the pattern."

Take the story of Cain and Abel. Cain brought of the fruit of the ground, an offering to the Lord. Abel brought a lamb. God rejected Cain's offering and accepted Abel's. So, at the very beginning of time, God showed the pattern that we must follow. The fruit of the ground is man's way of getting rid of sin and is rejected by God. The lamb, dying in our place, is God's way. Thousands of years later, Paul reiterated this pattern, *"Without the shedding of blood, there is no remission of sin."* (Hebrews 9:22, 11:4)

In Galatians 4:22, there's the story of Sarah and Hagar that emphasizes another pattern we must follow. Hagar had a son, Ishmael. Sarah had a son named Isaac. Ishmael was the product of a slave woman and of a natural, ordinary birth. Isaac was the product of a free woman, Abraham's wife, and the fulfillment of God's promise of a supernatural birth. Ishmael was rejected. Isaac was accepted. Paul says this is our pattern today. To be accepted in God's family, there must be a supernatural birth based on God's promise. John 1:1 says we can't be born of blood (parents), nor of the will of the flesh (our own efforts), nor of the will of man (the church or preacher). These are the natural ordinary ways of getting accepted by God, but they don't work. We must be born of the Spirit. (John 3:5 & 6) *"By grace are you saved, through faith, and that not of yourselves. It is the gift of God, not of works."* (Ephesians 2:8)

Another important pattern is the story of Israel leaving Egypt, wandering in the wilderness, entering the Promised Land, conquering seven powerful tribes, and finally becoming the mightiest nation on earth. This is not a perfect pattern, since it includes Israel's failures, but it gives an overall picture of the Christian life. The Israelites were slaves in Egypt for over 400 years. This represents us before salvation, slaves to Satan. God sent Moses to demand that the Pharaoh set them free. Pharaoh refused. God, by a display of supernatural power, forced him to set them free. This represents God sending Jesus to die for our sins and then raising Him from the dead. This forced Satan to give up his hold on us. Israel then went through the Red Sea on dry land. This represents the absolute end of Satan's power over us. They began their march to the land of promise. This represents our studying the Word, seeking God, and being disciplined. When they reached it, they refused to go in. This certainly represents what most of us do. We read the promises of God but fail to act on them. We fail to wholly follow the Lord. Israel paid dearly for their failure. They had to stay in the wilderness for 40 years. And of course, we pay dearly in too many ways to describe here. Finally, they're back and ready to obey God. They must cross the Jordan River. Jordan means death. For us, it means:

Entering the tight gate - Matthew 7:13
Choosing the narrow way - Matthew 7:14
Denying self - Matthew 16:24
Taking up the cross - Matthew 16:24
Being crucified with Christ - Galatians 2:20
Losing your life to find it - Matthew 16:25
Counting everything loss for Christ - Philippians 3:7
Pressing toward the mark - Philippians 3:14
Running that you may win the prize - 1 Corinthians 9:24

Taking on His yoke - Matthew 11:29

After they crossed the Jordan River, they had to fight the battle of Jericho, and against all odds, they won. They were now in the land of promise. The big promise was that they would always win if they obeyed Him. *"Every place that you go I will give you - but be sure to observe the law, to keep it and meditate on it day and night."* (Joshua 1:2-8) For us, it means we, like them, will have to face powerful enemies, but against all odds, we can win if we obey Him and abide in Him.

Matthew 25:34 - *"Then shall He say to them on His right* (true followers) *come - inherit the kingdom prepared for you."*

Hebrews 10:36 - *"After you have done the will of God, you will receive the promise."*
Revelation 2:10 - *"Be faithful and I will give you a crown of life."*

Revelation 2:27 - *"He that overcomes shall be a ruler."*

Ephesians 6:12 - *"The enemies we face are not flesh and blood, but spiritual wickedness."*

John lumped all sins together as the lust of the eye, of the flesh, and the pride of life. (1 John 2:16) These enemies of our soul, like Jericho, can only be defeated by the power of God. We can't do it on our own. Israel's next experience demonstrated this. Their second battle was with Ai. They were defeated. Joshua fell on his face and ripped his clothes, pleading with God to show him why they were defeated. God said, *"Get up. Israel has sinned. That's why you were defeated. Find out who sinned and punish him."* (Joshua 7:6) God will not be with you as long as there is sin in the camp!! They investigated and found that one of the warriors had stolen some valuables and he was severely punished. This is a powerful pattern for us to follow. If we sin, all the promises of God are cancelled until we deal with it. How do we deal with it? We follow John's instructions: *"Confess our sins. He is faithful and just to forgive us of our sins."* (1 John 1:9)

From then on, Israel won victory after victory until the whole land of promise was theirs. This is the pattern for us, but sadly how few fulfill it, but some do. He will have an overcoming people. They will be like Israel became, a city on a hill, the joy of the whole earth. I don't know about you, but as the song says, "O, I want to be in that number, when the saints go marching in."

## Paul, the Apostle

Acts 9:1 says, *"Saul, breathing out threatenings against the disciples - journeyed to Damascus. Suddenly a light shined round about him - he fell to the earth, he heard a voice, 'Why are you persecuting me?' Paul replied, "Who are you, Lord?"' The answer was, "I am Jesus." Paul asked, "Lord, what would you have me do?" The Lord told Paul to, "Arise, it shall be told you what you must do."*

This was, no doubt, the greatest conversion in history. Saul, the killer, became Paul, the Apostle, and writer of most of the New Testament letters. His story gives hope to all of us. No matter how wicked we think we have been (Paul was a murderer), there's hope. In many ways, Paul's life is a pattern for us. He was traveling to Damascus. One dictionary said that the word refers to very expensive cloth, that is woven in two sets of parallel threads, so as to give it a two-tone look. I see us before we're saved, rushing eagerly for a brighter, fancier, two-tone tomorrow, driven to get as much as possible out of this life because that's all there is. We come from animals and we will die as animals. We don't believe in an afterlife.

I was on such a road for quite a while and then, like Paul, I saw a great light (heard a good sermon). In a flash, I saw myself persecuting Jesus by the way I was living. Jesus said on the cross, "Forgive them. They don't know what they're doing." That was me until a sermon opened my eyes. Then, like Paul, I asked what I was supposed to do. I didn't get an answer like Paul did, but I knew, without a doubt, I had to change the way I was living, like 180°. At the time, I was playing in a dance band and thinking it was heaven. I gave it up in a hurry for something better. I started reading the Bible. It was just like God talking to me. It's a fact that when you're hooked on the Bible, you're hearing from God. I found Psalm 2 to be my experience. If you delight in God's Word, everything you do will prosper.

Paul went on to become God's greatest servant. He changed the course of history by leading millions from hell-bent sinners to heaven bound saints. None of us can equal his success, fame, or glory, but we can model our lives after his. He said in 1 Corinthians 11:1, *"Be followers of me as I am of Christ."* The verse that sums up his life best is Philippians 1:21, *"To me to live is Christ."* If you've heard someone say, "To me to live is dancing, sports, or whatever," you know what it means. In Colossians 3:4, Paul said something that should give us pause. *"When Christ, who is our life, shall appear, then shall we also appear with Him in glory."* This says to me that if Christ is our life (our everything), then shall we be caught up to be with Him in glory. Therefore, to quote Paul again, *"Forgetting those things that are behind and reaching forth unto those things which are before, let us press toward the goal, for the prize of the high calling of God."* (Philippians 3:14)

## Philosophy of Life

What is life all about? Life is about God's plan to have a family with every member made in His image and likeness. I believe everything that happens is designed to further His purpose. *" All things work together for good to them that love the Lord, who are called according to His purpose."* (Romans 8:28) The converse is also true. All things work together for evil to them that hate (ignore) the Lord and reject His purpose. I believe everything in this world is temporary except our souls and the Word of God. (Matthew 21:33) I see the world as the scaffolding in construction. When the building is finished, the scaffold is removed. God is using this world as the scaffolding. We are the building - a temple for Him to dwell in. *"You are built together for a habitation of God through the Spirit."* (Ephesians 2:22) You also might think of the world as a testing ground where they check out new weapons to see how they operate. People are placed in this world on probation and given a certain amount of time to prove what they're made of. Everything that happens to them is designed to reveal their character. And sad to say, most people are not interested in God's purpose. They will not acknowledge Him, except to tip their hat once in awhile, like at Christmas and Easter. They seem to have it good in this life, but all of a sudden, the curtain falls and the game is over. They will now stand before the judge. They might hear Him say, "Did you know the Bible says, *'Only a fool says there is no God'* (Psalm 14 :1) Or He might ask them, "Did you know Jesus asked this question, *What does it profit you to live it up for a short time and then lose your soul?'"* (Mark 8:6) Did you know that God so loved you that He gave His only Son so that you could be saved from sin and go to heaven? (John 3:16) *"As many as receive Christ become children of God."* (John 1:12) These are the verses you should build your life on, then you will hear God say, *"Well done good and faithful servant. Enter into the joy of the Lord."*

The Bible is God's message to people. They're supposed to read it, believe it, and obey it. If they ignore it, they would hear these words, *"Depart from me you workers of iniquity."* (Luke 13:27) God is creating a new human race, not like Adam, who was tested and failed, but like Christ, who was tested and overcame. Obviously not many will qualify to be in this new race. It might seem like the project is a failure, but God is not interested in quantity as much as in quality. He calls His people the remnant. The Bible says God's remnant will inherit the earth. (Romans 11:3-5)

Godly people are hard to find, even in some churches. Jesus predicted this. He said, *"Many are called* (all of us), *but few are chosen* (few choose to accept)." The ones who qualify will be blessed beyond their wildest dreams. The Apostle Paul said, *"Eye hath not seen nor ear heard, neither has it entered into the heart of man, the things which God has prepared for them that love Him."* (1 Corinthians 2:9)

Death is coming to every one of us. *"It is appointed unto man once to die, but after this, the judgment."* (Hebrews 9:27) It can be something to dread, or something to embrace. As long as we live, we can make our reservations either for a fiery hell or a beautiful heaven. *"Then I saw a new heaven and a new earth - I heard a voice saying, 'The house of God is now with men - He shall wipe away all tears, there shall be no more death, sorrow, or crying. He that overcomes* (sin) *shall inherit all things.'"*(Revelation 21:1-7) This is the only true philosophy of life. Anything else is a philosophy of death.

## Psalm 2 (What's Going On In The World?)

You need to see the big picture to understand what is going on in the world. The Bible has all the answers and it behooves everybody to read it if they want to be prepared for what is coming. The Lord has given us in Psalm 2 a brief and concise explanation of what is going on. Turn to it and you will see that there are twelve verses divided into four groups of three each. In each group, someone is making a statement. Each someone is a key player on the world stage. The first speaker is most people of the world. The second speaker is God, the third is Jesus, and the fourth is the Holy Spirit.

In the first three verses, the people of the world are saying as strongly as possible that they reject Christ. Notice the violent language, "Let us bust up their churches and get rid of all their teachings." This has already taken place in Russia, and in many other countries. The U.S., in an official sense, has rejected Christ.

In the second group of verses, God is speaking. First, He laughs. It's like a worm telling a man to get lost. But then, God speaks in anger saying, "In spite of the problems you have with my Son, He will become King over all the earth."

In the next three verses, Christ is speaking. He says, *"The Lord has said unto me, you are my son. This day have I begotten you."* Then He says, *"Ask of me and I will give you the whole world for your possession. You shall break them with a rod of iron. You shall dash them in pieces."* Pretty strong words!

In the last three verses the Holy Spirit says, *"Be wise, you kings and you judges. Kiss the Son,* meaning make peace with Him. He urges all people to use their heads and take the warning seriously. If they accept the Son, they will be saved. If they reject the Son, they will suddenly be destroyed.

The missing player in this scenario is Satan, the arch enemy of God. He is in the back of man's rebellion. Most people, as indicated in the first three verses, reject God's Savior. They prefer to remain in Satan's camp. Sadly, they will end up in the hell that was prepared for Satan and his angels.

This is the big picture of what's going on. All the wars, floods, earthquakes, famines, diseases, etc., are part of the picture. Jesus said in John 10:10 that Satan's purpose is to steal, kill, and destroy. Since most of the people in the world are on Satan's side, that's what is happening. The tragedy of 9/11 is a sample of Satan's work. In Luke 13:4, a tower fell and killed 18 people. The disciples asked if it was because they were really bad sinners. Jesus said no. We're all sinners and scheduled to die. It is not terribly important when we die, but it is crucially important where we go. Jesus made it as plain as possible that if we don't repent and follow Him, we will go to the wrong place, which is infinitely worse than just dying.

## Pure As Solid Gold

*"When He has examined me, He will pronounce me as pure as solid gold.* (Job 23:10) The Psalmist says, *"Thank you for making me so wonderfully complex. It is amazing to think about. Your workmanship is*

*marvelous and how well I know it. You were there while I was being formed in secret. You saw me before I was born and scheduled each day of my life.* (Psalm 19:11)

Think for a minute about your body. It is a million times more complicated than the great City of New York. Your nervous system is a million times more complicated than all the electric and telephone wires in New York. Your digestive tubes are a million times more complicated than all the water pipes, sewer pipes, and gas pipes in New York. Your circulatory system is a million times more complicated than the transportation system - roads, bridges, tunnels, etc., in New York. Your brain is a million times more complicated than all the computers, etc., in New York. Your sensory system is a million times more complicated than all the sensors they have in New York. Your eyeball is a million times more complicated than the best video cameras in New York. The immune system that protects you is a million times more efficient than all the police, firemen, and security systems in New York. Your self-healing power is greater than all the doctors and hospital personnel in New York. Your heart is a million times more complicated than all the power and pumping stations in New York. Your stomach is a million times more complicated than all the chemical plants in New York. And on it goes.

For another illustration, think of some boss telling you to feed every person in New York City a full course meal. Think of the logistics, of the number of workers you'd need, of the transportation, of the cleanup. You would rightly throw up your hands and say, "Impossible!" This is what God is doing in your body every day, all the time (and in everyone else's body). Millions and millions of cells are clamoring to be fed. God supplies the necessary food and oxygen. The blood picks them up from the small intestines and from the lungs, and then delivers them to every cell through myriads of arteries, capillaries, and veins. This goes on continuously. Now, multiply this by some huge number and you have a little idea of the complexity, the exquisite precision, and miraculous industry that is found in your body. Can you believe that all this is for nothing?

For another illustration, think of the exact fits in the body. Anyone who makes things knows how hard it is to make things fit. In fact, just think how hard it is to get a good fit in clothes. Now think of the parts of the body. There's a song about the bones being joined together. The foot bones joined to the ankle bone, etc. Every joint has to be perfect or we'd be in trouble. Tell a pipe fitter how easy his job is, and he'd laugh. Our bodies would be a pipe fitter's nightmare with all the intestines, the arteries, veins and capillaries, the trachea, the esophagus, etc., etc. They all have to be exactly the right size and length. Now think of the organs that fit in the abdominal cavity. Everyone has to be exactly the right size for its job. Think of the arms and legs on the right and left side of the body being exactly the same; the eyes, ears, hands, shoulders, etc. Think of the teeth. If they were the slightest bit off, they wouldn't work. Now to stretch your mind, think of the trillions of atoms that make up the body. Each one is custom made for its job. Each one is where it's supposed to be. All the engineers in the world couldn't make such a masterpiece.

The point is you were created as a greater entity than any man-made thing on this earth. We haven't even mentioned soul and spirit, which would take up too much time for this article. Now think of the purpose of such a creation. Could it be trivial or would it have to be deadly serious? Is New York City a trivial thing? As the business capital of the world, it keeps wheels turning everywhere. It's certainly not trivial. You couldn't possibly say to New York, "Take a year off. Shut down everything and enjoy!" There would be chaos. Now, try to realize that you are more important than New York City. Does that give you some idea how important you are, how deadly serious your life is, or do you see yourself as a mere trifle in the big scheme of things; a cog in the wheel that's going nowhere? If this is your assessment of yourself, you've missed the point of your creation. You can be sure, God never created such a being as you are for a frivolous purpose. He intends to show you off to the universe, not for a day, but for eternity (Ephesians 3:10). Will you frustrate this purpose? If you take the low view, you will grieve the Lord, but if you reach for the stars, you're the very one He's looking for. *"The eyes of the Lord run to and fro throughout the whole earth to show Himself strong on behalf of the one whose heart is perfect toward Him."* (2 Chronicles 16:9) God says he will make a man more precious than a wedge of pure gold. (Isaiah 13:12) He doesn't mean literal gold, but what it represents, i.e., without price character that spreads its influence far and wide. You are to be *"the love of God shed abroad."* (Romans 5:5)

This article is supposed to help you realize the incalculable value of a human being. Jesus said, *"What shall it profit a man if he gains the whole world and loses his soul, or what shall a man give in exchange for his soul."* (Matthew 16:26) One soul is worth more than the whole world. God has a huge investment in us, and He expects a return on his investment. Luke 13:6 tells of a fig tree that didn't bear fruit for three years. The Lord said, "Cut it down." It's incumbent on us to become the gold God is seeking, or to suffer great loss.

## Rags to Riches

As a boy, my favorite books were the ones written by Horatio Alger. One of them had the title I've chosen for this article. It was the story of a poor boy who worked hard and went from poverty to great wealth. It must have had some effect on me, as I, more or less, followed the same path.

Growing up in the depression was tough. Everybody was poor, and it took a miracle to get a job. After high school, the best offer I got was to be a pan greaser in a bakery at 40 cents an hour. I worked there six years without even a nickel raise. At least they promoted me to another machine. A union was formed and promised us more money, but instead, the bakery closed up.

I went into construction work for almost ten years and made more money, but it was back-breaking work, and to me, it seemed like a dead-end job. All this time, I was taking college courses, hoping they would lead me out of the wilderness. Eventually, I had my degree and with it, the offer of a teaching position. It took a while, but I finally had a job I loved. The money wasn't that great, but the amenities were wonderful (summer vacation)! By the grace of God, I had gone from rags to riches.

It was good to become rich in this materialistic sense. Incidentally, everyone should know that the poorest in this country is very rich, compared to the rest of the world. However, the point I want to make in this article is about going from rags to riches in the spiritual world, which is a million times more important and rewarding than the materialistic world.

I realized early on that I was anything but a role model. I was definitely in the rags class when it came to behavior, but I did go to church. Once in a while I picked up something that piqued my curiosity. Our preacher expounded on John 1:12, "*As many as received Him (Jesus), God gave the power to become sons of God.*" Who wouldn't want to be a son of God? So, I received Him and for years I enjoyed my new status, but one day, I happened on Romans 8:14, "*As many as are led by the Spirit of God, they are the sons of God!*" This put a new light on the subject: Maybe I wasn't a son after all. How is one led by the Spirit? To make a very long story short, I learned that the verse doesn't say we become sons of God, but we receive power to become sons of God. I found a verse that says we start the Christian life as babies. As we read the Word of God, we grow and if we keep on reading, we will become sons of God (1 Peter 2:2). The Holy Spirit and Word are one and the same, so it follows that the more you get in the Word, the more you are led by the Spirit. I got in the Word big time and found the Lord leading me in many ways. In fact, in a short while, He led me from the rags of this anti-God world, to the riches of living in Christ and having Christ living in me. As Paul said in Acts 17:28, "*In Him I live and move and have my being.*" "*For me to live is Christ.*" (Philippians 1:21) Paul says it best, "*Godliness is profitable unto all things, having promise of the life that now is and of that which is to come.*" (1 Timothy 4:8)

# Rock of Ages

As you will see, there are some real gems in our hymnology and one of the brightest is my article title.

Rock of ages cleft for me, let me hide myself in thee.
Let the water and the blood, from thy wounded side
which flowed,
Be of sin the double cure, save from wrath and make me
pure.

This one verse of a song says it all in just two sentences. Amazing! The composer begins with the word 'rock', an important word in the Bible. Way back in Exodus, God is portrayed as a rock. God told Moses to bring water out of the rock for the people in the wilderness. *"You shall smite the rock and water shall come out of it."* (Exodus 17:6) This was a prophecy of the future redemption of the people. The rock is Christ, the smiting is the crucifixion, and the water is the outpouring of God's Spirit on the Day of Pentecost. Later, in Exodus 33:21, Moses asked the Lord if he would show him His glory. God said, *"You shall stand upon a rock --- and while my glory passes by, I will put you in a cleft of the rock."* This is another prophecy of a future redemption. The cleft in the rock would be Jesus crucified. Remember, Jesus was pierced with a spear and blood and water came out (John 19:34). The blood symbolizes salvation, and the water represents sanctification. *"That He might sanctify and cleanse us with the washing of water by the Word."* (Ephesians 5:26) David knew these scriptures. He said, *"The Lord is my rock and my fortress and my deliverer, my God, in whom I will trust."* (Psalm 18:2) Paul refers to those Old Testament days. *"They did all drink of that spiritual rock that followed them and that rock was Christ."* (1 Corinthians 10:4)

A rock is certainly a good symbol of Christ. He was like the Rock of Gibraltar, unmovable, in the carrying out of His purpose. (Isaiah 50:7) Another important reference to the Rock is found in Song of Solomon 2:14. The Lord is speaking in verse 10, saying, *"O, my dove, in the cleft of the rock, in the secret of the stairs, let me see your face and hear your voice.*" Dove refers to God's people. They are found in the cleft of the rock, i.e., their faith was in Jesus who was wounded for them. And that is the 'secret of the stairs', which is the secret of access to God, the secret of growing in grace and in knowledge of the spiritual life, and the secret of entering the pearly gates.

'Be of sin the double cure. Save from wrath and make me pure.' These words are so important. Many people I talk to believe they are saved from the wrath of God because they go to church. That's a possibility if they truly repent of their sins and ask Jesus to come into their heart (Luke 13:3 and John 1:12), but to be sure of heaven, we need the double cure: salvation and purity. Of course, we are made pure when we are saved, but it doesn't last. Remember when Jesus washed the disciples' feet? Peter said, *"Wash me all over."* Jesus replied, "*He that is washed* [saved] *needs not but to wash his feet."* (John 13:9 & 10) In other words, we live in a dirty world and we will get dirty no matter how hard we try to stay clean. The secret to staying clean is found in 1 John 1:9, *"If we confess our sins, He is faithful and just to forgive us our sins and to cleanse us from all unrighteousness."* Using this verse every day means the difference between life and death. Right here and right now is the time to get rid of sin. There will be no purgatory or second chance after you die. Remember, life is short, eternity is long!

## Subterfuge

Subterfuge is a sort of minor deceit, or cover up, that is done in secret to save face, or possibly criticism. The one that comes to mind first is the story of Ananias and Sapphira in Acts 5. They sold some property ostensibly to give the proceeds to the church, but foolishly, they decided to keep some of it for themselves. If they had just been open about it, there would have been no problem, but they wanted credit for the whole amount when that wasn't what was given. It must be something God hates very much, since they both died as soon as they opened their mouths.

In Genesis 20:2, Abraham told the king of a country he was visiting that Sarah, his wife, was his sister. She was his half-sister, so it was partly true, but the Lord was not at all pleased with this subterfuge. Genesis 32 tells the story of Israel losing faith in Moses because he stayed on the mountain so long, and so they told Aaron to make a god for them. He made a golden calf. Later when Moses was charging him with sin he said, "*I cast their gold into the fire and out came this calf.*" (Verse 24) What a subterfuge. Three thousand died for that escapade!

Jesus said, "*In the last days, false prophets shall rise - shall seduce, if it were possible, the very elect.*" They do it by half-truths that are difficult to detect. In John 1:47, Jesus saw Nathanael and said of him, "*Behold an Israelite indeed in whom is no guile.*" The fact that this impressed Him says a lot about the general population. In fact, Jesus told what He thought of the general population in John 2:24-25, "*Jesus did not commit Himself unto them because He knew all men and needed not that any man should testify of man for He knew what was in Man!*" What an indictment, and not to heathens, but to God's own people!

These examples certainly should give us pause. Revelation 21:11 gives us some light on this subject, "*The holy Jerusalem - was like unto a - jasper stone clear as crystal.*" Verse 18 says, "*The city was like unto clear glass.*" It's repeated in verse 21. This indicates that everyone in heaven will be transparent. There will be no subterfuges.

"*We shall be like Him for we shall see Him as He is. And every man that has this hope purifies himself even as He is pure.*" (1 John 3:2 & 3)

# Suffering

I never thought much about suffering until one day I read Romans 8:17, *"We are joint heirs of God if we suffer with Him."* The 'if' in the verse makes it a conditional promise. Becoming an heir of Christ depends on our suffering with Him. This doesn't have anything to do with salvation, since salvation is a free gift, *"not of works, lest any man should boast"* (Ephesians 2:9); so it must have to do with our level of commitment after we're saved. The question is, what does suffering mean and what does joint heir mean? Jesus does say we will suffer persecution. *"Blessed are you when men shall hate you. Rejoice, for your reward is great."* (Luke 6:22) The problem, if it can be called a problem, is that in America we are not called on to suffer. Many parts of the world are suffering intense persecution. Ethnic cleansing is going on all over, but so far, we've been spared.

There is an aspect of suffering that is more likely to be what Paul is talking about, which is to enter into Christ's sufferings, to ask the Lord to open our spiritual eyes to how terribly Jesus suffered to redeem us. Paul said in Philippians 3:10, *"O that I might know Him – the fellowship of His suffering, being made conformable to His death."* *"Christ suffered for us, leaving us an example that we should follow in His steps."* (1 Peter 2:21) The description of the crucifixion in the gospels is very brief. We must fill in the gaps, see the nails being hammered into His hands and feet, realizing that He was taking the pain.

I was in extreme pain a couple times in my life. Once a shark crunched down on my foot. Yes, a shark. His teeth went right to the bone and I nearly fainted with the pain. He let go, since it wasn't the ham bone he was hoping for, and I came to in time to kick and scream and get away. It took 36 stitches to close-up all the punctures. That hurt for several days, and then to top it off, about a week later, I was going through a door with a strong spring to it. Being clumsy with my crutches, it sprang back and hit my sore foot. I can tell you, I wanted to die. I believe the Lord told me right then, that this was a sample of what He suffered. He also reminded me that it was my sins that caused His suffering. From then on, whenever I meditated on His sufferings, I thought of my sore foot. Of course, it's nothing compared to His suffering, but I got the idea. As the song goes, "I can never, never tell you what He's done for me."

Another aspect of suffering is the opposition of the world to the gospel. The world, inspired by the devil, hates God and everything connected with God. He instigates all the evil. He even gets religious people to murder. It was the religious who plotted to kill Jesus many times, and finally succeeded. Followers of Christ will be persecuted. *"But rejoice inasmuch as you are partakers of Christ's sufferings."* (1 Peter 5:10) *"Unto you it is given in the behalf of Christ, not only to believe on Him, but also to suffer for His sake."* (Philippians 1:29) *"They rejoiced that they were counted worthy to suffer shame for His name."* (Acts 5:41)

When Paul was saved, the Lord said, *"I will show him how great things he must suffer for my name's sake."* (Acts 9:16) Paul was the preeminent sufferer. The description of his sufferings in 2 Corinthians 11:23-30 is awesome. Jesus, Paul, and many others suffered because they were aggressive in preaching the gospel. Most of us are not even active, we're passive, so we will never suffer persecution. In that case, we have to accept the words of our text: *"If we suffer with Him, we will be heirs of Christ."* If we don't suffer with Him, we will suffer loss.

About joint heirs, to be an heir is to inherit something. Jesus said, *"The meek shall inherit the earth."* (Matthew 5:5) He said in Revelation 3:21, that overcomers will sit with Him on His throne. The reward or suffering with Him is utterly fantastic, and as Paul says in Romans 8:18, *"The sufferings of this present time are not worthy to be compared with the glory that shall be revealed in us."*

# Testing

It's déjà vu time! I thought I was home free; no more hospitals, no more trials of my faith, but I was wrong. I woke up on December 30 with my right arm sound asleep. I began to rub it with no results. Then Gerry and I both rubbed it with no results. I got up and my arm was dangling like a piece of wood, with no feeling and no control. You can believe I was shocked. I knew this was no bump in the road. I thought it was the beginning of the end. Gerry thought I'd had a stroke and felt we needed to get to the hospital as soon as possible. She knew there was a three-hour window where you could get a shot, if you have had a stroke, which would counteract at least part of the damage. We rushed to Christiana Hospital full speed, where they put me through the alphabet tests: CAT, EKG, MRI, a carotid ultrasound, and more. I was not a candidate for the shot because of my age and because we did not have a definite onset time. The next day, the neurologist came in and said it was a stroke, but not the irreversible kind. Later when another doctor came in, he said it was a mild stroke, but I would need to go to a rehab for at least a week for therapy. He said one of my carotid arteries was 50% blocked. I couldn't hear everything they said, so I probably lost some more of my hearing too.

Meantime, my arm was coming back to life. By Saturday morning, New Year's Day, I was telling the doctors I was healed, and I felt like a miracle had taken place. After some discussion, surprise, surprise, they agreed that I could go home. I was one happy camper! I was singing, "There's no place like home for New Year's Day," and there's nothing like having an arm that works.

As usual in these matters, I was wondering what the Lord was telling me. At first, I focused on the right arm. Is there anything significant about that? I use my right arm for writing. Am I taking credit that belongs to God alone? I often say, "Nothing in my hand I bring, simply to the cross I cling." I felt the answer was no. The element of surprise is taught throughout the Bible, but it surely doesn't hurt to have a reminder. Jesus is coming as a thief in the night (2 Peter 3:10).

That could mean coming for us in the rapture or coming for us in death. We shouldn't really be surprised at anything that happens to us. If we're in touch with the Lord at all times, we'll be prepared. Read how God helped Paul. (Acts 27:21- 24) So one lesson is plain; be ready at all times, even moment by moment.

Secondly, when I thought my arm was gone for good, I was devastated. I could only think of my loss. No more writing and as for the piano, forget it. I confessed that my faith was weak, and I affirm that I've been forgiven now. (1 John 1:9) I've also been impressed with the need to give thanks to the Lord for everything, not to take anything for granted. (Ephesians 5:20) We are His masterpiece, made in His image and likeness. O, give Him thanks!

A third lesson could be to realize how fragile we are. Any minute a little speck can clog and stop the flow of blood to the brain and our lives are drastically changed or even ended. That again, says we should be ready always. I'm now making it a practice to say, "My health is in You, Lord."

A fourth lesson we could get from the sudden death syndrome is that, at best, we only have a short time to spend here on earth. James 4:4 says, *"Your life is a vapor that appears for a little time and then vanishes away."* We need to know that this is preparation time for the next life. We're supposed to rule and reign with Christ - to be part of His administration. (Revelation 5:10) It takes a lot of time to prepare for such responsibilities. It's the same as in our natural life. To be really good at anything takes a long time, and likewise, to be spiritually mature takes time. I thank the Lord every day that He got me started at an early age, and if I've been careless and needed this nudge, I thank the Lord for it.

What it all boils down to is this: Judgment Day is coming. Christ's return is an instant judgment. To help us understand this, Jesus told a parable about ten virgins waiting for a wedding. Five were wise, and five were foolish. (Matthew 25) The wise had plenty of oil, a type of the Holy Spirit. The foolish were just about out of oil. The wedding suddenly started. The wise went in, but the foolish were unprepared, so the door was shut, and they were left out. The Bible doesn't say they didn't have any oil. They didn't have enough. This should make us stop and think. Is our maturity level where it needs to be? Are we filled with the Holy Spirit? Are we spending time with the Lord and growing in Him Time is short? When He comes for us, either in the Rapture or in death, we can't say, "Just let me have one more day to get ready."

## The Body as an Object Lesson

In thinking about the complexity of the body, I'm led to say that if our bodies were the only proof for the existence of God, it would be enough for me. There's no way something so complicated could be an accident, but the big lesson about our bodies is not how wonderful they are, but how they are made to fit into and become part of another body. That other body is the body of Christ. 1 Corinthians 12:12-27 tells us that each of us is a part of His body. We have been baptized into Christ's body by the Holy Spirit. Every part is important. If the foot says, "I am not a part of the body because I'm not a hand," that does not make it any less a part of the body. God has put each part (you and I) where He wants us. The parts that seem least important may be the most necessary. If one part suffers, they all suffer. If one part is honored, all parts rejoice. Paul goes on to describe the different parts and their function. For example, a preacher could be the mouth in Christ's body, a prophet could be the eyes, etc. You may say, "I'm just a toe." If this is God's will, be glad and rejoice in it.

One more consideration, your body is not yours on two counts. First, your body is God's. He created it and He owns it. You have it on loan from Him. It is to house your soul, which is on probation for your brief time on earth. Second, you are not your own, because you were bought with a price, the blood of Jesus. Let us acknowledge these truths and God will bless us. "*In all your ways acknowledge Him and He will direct your steps.*" (Proverbs 3:6)

The body is a huge object lesson. Paul says, "*God gave Jesus to be the head of the church, which is His body.*" (Ephesians 1:22) "*We are to grow up into Him, which is the head, from whom the whole body fitly joined together, each part helping the other parts so that the whole body is healthy and growing in love.*" (Ephesians 4:16).

The torso is under the control of the head. When the head says run, swim, wrestle, walk, or throw, the parts obey. If any part doesn't function it is considered paralyzed and must be examined and given proper treatment. In some cases, limbs have to be amputated, so that the rest of the body isn't affected.

It's the same way with the Spiritual body. When a Christian doesn't hear the Lord's voice and doesn't obey, it's a very serious matter that must be taken care of, lest the rest of the body is affected. Paul, in 1 Corinthians 5, had to deal with this problem. One of the members got into serious sin. Paul used another object lesson to explain the situation. He said, "Don't you know a little leaven leavens the whole loaf?" In other words, the whole church will be affected. "Purge out the leaven - remove the wicked person so that you will stay healthy."

Another example is found in Galatians 4:19, "*My little children, of whom I travail in birth again, until Christ be formed in you.*" Here it sounds like Paul isn't sure these people are part of the body yet. In verse 20 he says, "*I stand in doubt of you.*" In verse 16 he says, "*Obey the Holy Spirit's instructions. He will tell you where to go and what to do.*" In other words, to be a part of the functioning body of Christ, you must be yielded to the Holy Spirit.

Jesus said in John 10:27, "*My sheep* (my body) *hear my voice, and they follow me* (obey)." It's quite plain. You are either hearing His voice (reading the Bible) and obeying it, and are, therefore, in the body, or you are not hearing His voice (not reading the Bible) or obeying it, and are, therefore, not in the body. If you are in the body and growing in grace, you will end up fulfilling Romans 8:29, *"For whom He did foreknow, He also did predestinate to be conformed to the image of His Son, that he might be the firstborn among many brethren."*

## The Cross

Some time ago when Mel Gibson's film "The Passion of the Christ" was released, the whole world took a second look at the crucifixion scene. It is said a picture is worth more than a thousand words. Billy Graham said that one film was worth a lifetime of sermons. There is no doubt that the world got its first graphic, heart wrenching, understanding of the price Jesus paid to free people from their sins. Only perfect, agape (unconditional) love could enable Jesus to bear such brutal torture for us. We need to remember that He did it for His enemies, as well as for His friends. His last words were, *"Father, forgive them!"*

The cross was probably the cruelest execution ever devised. God purposely allowed it because it was peculiarly suited to fit the crimes that Jesus was dying for. More on that later, but God wants us to fully understand the enormity of sin. The world jokes about sin, but God hates it with such a passion that He was willing to give His beloved Son; first, to show us the horrendous consequences of sin, and second, to stamp it out. In the Garden of Gethsemane, Jesus asked three times if there was another way, but God let him know unless He took our sins and our death penalty, we would be destroyed. When Jesus considered this, He began to sweat blood. This was just a glimpse of the agony He was going through. Most people think the cup Jesus was to drink was His fear of death. This could not be. It had to be His revulsion, His horror of actually becoming the sin that He hated, as well as having His Father forsake Him. Just think of Jesus becoming the worst monster like Hitler, Stalin, or Saddam Hussein. This is what caused His blood vessels to rupture. (2 Cor. 5:21)

Not too long ago, whole herds of cattle and thousands of chickens had to be destroyed for having a disease. Everybody understands this. Without immediate action, thousands, maybe millions of people would be at risk. This is the situation with sin. It is a deadly disease. It has spread all over the world and there is no cure. The penalty of death must be carried out. This is a spiritual law as irrevocable and unchanging as the law of gravity. Jesus knew He was the only one who could save mankind. His perfect life qualified Him to take our place and pay our penalty. He then could be raised to life again, since Satan had no claim on Him. We should thank God every day, that Jesus was able to say, *"Not my will but thine be done."*

As mentioned earlier, the cross is peculiarly suited to express the wrath of God upon each part of the body that was involved in sin and rebellion. It is a huge object lesson to the world that, sadly, is too little understood. You must keep in mind as you read on, that the punishment inflicted on Jesus was designed for sinners (you and me). It is a very graphic and terrible picture of the consequences of rebelling against God.

Notice that the feet are singled out for punishment. There was much concern in Bible days about having clean feet. Think of the King of the Universe stooping so low as to wash the disciples' feet. The feet were supposed to do good. Isaiah 52:7 says, *"How beautiful are the feet of him that brings good tidings."* But then, Proverbs 1:16 says, *"Their feet run to do evil."* Romans 3:15 says, *"Their feet are swift to shed blood."* Isaiah 53:6 says, *"We all have turned to walk in our own way."* It was a fit punishment for feet to be nailed.

The hands are such an indispensable part of the body, having the ability to do much good, not just for ourselves, but for others. They are used also in showing friendship and in the worship of God. Jesus touched people and they were healed. But, Micah 7:3 says, *"They do evil with both hands earnestly."* In John 19:3, they smote Jesus with their hands. Revelation 9:20 says, *"They repented not of the work of their hands."* It was fitting that the hands should be nailed.

136

Notice the case against the mind, once the most wonderful part of the body. But the part that distinguishes us from animals became the part that made us worse than animals. It totally rejects God. *"God is not in all their thoughts."* (Psalm 10:4) *"It is the enemy of God."* (Romans 8:7) In many verses, it is described as corrupt, blinded, reprobate, and totally depraved. *"Every imagination of the thoughts of men is only evil, continually."* (Gen. 6:5) What an indictment! Of course, our eyes and ears we have closed, lest we see and hear and understand God's call to us. It is well deserved that the head should be pierced with many thorns.

The face is the visible expression of the heart. It is supposed to show the glory of God as did Moses coming down from the mountain. But, instead we read, *"They have made their faces harder than a rock."* (Jeremiah 5:3) *They hid their faces from Him* (Jesus). *They spit in His face.* (Matthew 26:67) It is a well-deserved punishment that the soldiers should spit in the face. (Isaiah 50:6)

The beard is supposed to be a sign of maturity, but man, long ago, forfeited any claim to maturity. Jesus focused on it when he said, *"You're just like children. John came neither eating or drinking and you said he was a devil. I came eating and drinking and you say I'm a drunkard."* It was well-deserved that the beard should be plucked out. (Isaiah 50:6)

The back is a symbol of strength. A man is praised for having a backbone. In the beginning, God made man upright. *"The upright are His delight."* (Proverbs 5:18) *But man chose to turn away.* (Ecclesiastes 7:29) Micah 7:2 tells us, *"There is not one upright among men."* Psalm 44:25 says, *"Your soul is bowed down to the dust."* Isaiah 2:9 and 46:2 say, *"They stoop, they bow down to idols."* It was a righteous thing that the back should be scourged with many stripes.

The heart keeps us alive physically and spiritually. Out of the heart are the issues of life: our emotions, conscience, affections, and desires. *"Guard your heart - set your affections on things above,"* says the Bible. But man rejected this advice and let the heart run wild and become vain, darkened, vile, proud, sensuous, deceitful above all things, and desperately wicked. It was fitting that a spear should be thrust through the heart.

Isaiah 53 is called the Calvary of The Old Testament. Here we read of Jesus being wounded for our transgressions, bruised for our iniquities, chastised for our peace, and beaten for our healing. Isaiah 52:14 tells us that Jesus was marred (beaten) more than any man. People who saw Him were appalled. But God looked upon the suffering of His Son and was satisfied. (Isaiah 53:11) How could God be satisfied?

Because God's people, whom He loved, were saved from destruction. To use the vernacular, Jesus got us off the hook. He took what we deserved - paid our debt in full. Everyone who desires to be in God's family is now welcomed simply by receiving Jesus as Savior. *"When you make His soul an offering for sin, He will see His children."* (Isaiah 53:10) The human race was saved (all who respond to His offer).

Friend, I responded to His offer. I'll be the first to admit that my feet went astray; they ran to do evil. My hands became fists more than once; they took things belonging to somebody else. My face leered at the goody goodies. My heart ran wild for too many years. I let the "evil birds" build a nest in my mind. Even now, as a Christian, my backbone is more like a wet noodle. But, because of the cross, all that is behind me. I say with Paul, *"I am crucified with Christ."* (Galatians 2:20) The parts of my body that served Satan died on the cross. They have been resurrected to serve God. (Romans 6:19) Now, here is the crucial point. If you accept God's offer but continue in sin, you're wasting your time. You're either a new creation or you're still in sin. (2 Corinthians 5:17) If you still feel the pull of the world, you need to realize that the carnal mind is death. Only the mind controlled by the Spirit leads to eternal life. (Romans 8:6)

Consider what I say and the Lord give you understanding in all things. (2 Tim 2:7) The hymn says, "Jesus paid it all. All to Him I owe. Sin had left a crimson stain. He washed it white as snow."

## The Fall and Rise of Man

God's greatest creation is not this universe of sun, moon, stars, planets, and earth; it is the people He made to live here. He formed it to be inhabited. (Isaiah 45:18) Jesus said that one soul is worth more than the whole earth. (Mark 8:36-37) God's purpose is to have children in His image; the same purpose that every family has.

So, God made Adam and Eve. He gave them one easy test to prove them and warned them they would die if they disobeyed. They failed the test. Immediately, they knew they were undone. Everything was changed. When the Lord came to visit, they hid. When they looked at themselves, they were ashamed. When God asked them what happened, they stonewalled. Adam blamed Eve. Eve blamed Satan. They never thought to say, "We're sorry." Fellowship, trust, and pleasures were gone. Fear came. They knew their creator could snuff out their lives in a moment. God's holiness and justice automatically condemns rebellion to instant death, so man died, spiritually first, and physically later. The world and they, themselves, would henceforth live in a pit of ruination and destruction. This proved true very quickly. Their first child became a murderer.

Although God is perfectly just, He also is perfect love, and fortunately for us (as Adam's children), He had a contingency plan. Right after telling Adam and Eve the consequences of their failure, God announced His purpose to restore them. First, He killed animals to show them that disobedience results in death. Then, He clothed them with the animals' skins. In Genesis 3:15, He said the seed (child) of a woman would someday come and destroy their adversary, Satan, and restore the human family to God's favor. God had to do the unthinkable: let His son become a human and let Him take man's sins and death penalty on Himself. *"He was slain from the foundation of the world."* (Revelation 13:8) God accomplished this by the greatest object lesson ever devised. He took the Roman Empire the most advanced of all governments, and Israel, the most advanced, and in fact, only true religion, and let them demonstrate for all time, the desperately wicked nature of man. They conspired together to nail the Son of God to a cross. Satan, of course, was the instigator. He never realized that by destroying Jesus, he was destroying himself. Every member of the human family can now be free from Satan's control by simply saying, "Jesus paid my debt."

With the crucifixion of Jesus, mankind has a pardon for sin, but here is the saddest part of the story. Most people who call themselves Christians think that joining a church saves them, or they pray to Mary and the other Saints, or worst of all, they think that the big money they give will save them. All of this is strong delusion. Paul said only one thing will save you, and that is you have to become a totally new and different person. (Galatians 6:15) He says again in 2 Corinthians 5:17, *"If any man is in Christ, he is a brand-new person. Old things are passed away, all things are become new."* Before, you ignored God, now He is your life. Before, you loved sin, now you hate it. Anything less than this and you will hear Him say at the judgment, *"I never knew you."* (Matthew 7:21-23)

Salvation is like the gift of a check. If you don't cash it, it's worthless. How do you cash the salvation check? You hear that Jesus died for your sins. You believe it. You repent of your sins and receive Him as your Savior. (John 1:12)

Peter, in 1 Peter 2:2, compares a new Christian (and old ones too), to a newborn baby that desires and requires milk. The milk the Christian must have is the Word of God. If you have no desire, you are stillborn, meaning still lost. Peter again says, *"Give diligently* (work hard) *to make your calling and election sure."* (2 Peter 1:10)

# Types

Practically everything in the world has a Spiritual lesson for us. Jesus constantly pointed out the meaning of things, especially in parables. In Matthew 13, he told about a farmer planting seeds, some in good ground, and some in bad. In due time, he looked for a crop. The bad ground produced nothing. The good ground had mixed results, some yielding 30%, some 60%, and some 100%. The farmer is the Christian witnessing to someone. The ground is someone's heart. The seed is the Word of God. The bad ground people won't receive the gospel, so they can't produce anything, i.e. none of them get saved. The good ground people get saved, but with different levels of commitment; some with less than 50%, some with a little more than 50%, and some with 100% commitment.

Then Jesus tells of a field that had a lot of weeds mixed in with the wheat. The weeds are the unbelievers, and the wheat is the true believers. In the same chapter, he speaks of how yeast gradually affects the whole batch of dough. This is a prophecy that the whole world will gradually become totally wicked. This agrees with Matthew 24:37, "*As it was in the days of Noah, so shall it be when Christ returns,*" in other words, totally wicked.

Matthew 13:44 tells of a man finding treasure in a field and then buying that field to get it. This parable has a wonderful meaning. The field is the world. The treasure is the saved of all the ages. God was willing to pay the price to have a people for His name (Acts 15:14). The next verse in Matthew 13 speaks of a business man that paid a high price for a pearl. The pearl is significant in the Bible. Like the treasure in the field it represents the saved of all the ages, but in this case, it points out the distinguishing characteristic of God's people. Brace yourself as this may give you a jolt. The pearl, as you probably know, is formed in an oyster. Something like a grain of sand irritates the oyster, which then begins to secrete a substance on it. This process continues until a beautiful, valuable pearl is produced. Now turn to

Revelation 21:21 and see that the twelve gates to the New Jerusalem are pearls.

Do you think maybe God is telling us that we must cover everyone that irritates us with love, patience, etc.? Just a thought.

## Weeds

Genesis 3:18 says, *"Cursed is the ground. Thorns - shall it bring forth."* God is speaking of both physical and spiritual thorns. No one ever plants weeds and thorns. They are part of the curse. They grow naturally. Anybody that wants a garden had better start killing weeds, not just once in a while, but many times. Weeds are not good for looks or for food. In fact, they are hurtful. They are a waste. They take up room for nothing. The case against spiritual weeds is even worse. They grow naturally all right, but they also seem to grow exponentially. They spread much faster and further than physical weeds. Everyone recognizes physical weeds and there is a constant and universal effort to kill them, but spiritual weeds are not so easily recognized by most people and there is little effort to kill them.

The contrast between spiritual weeds and spiritual plants is found throughout the Bible. The first person born in the world had a weed of rebellion growing in him, and when the Lord gave him a command, he refused to obey. When he saw his younger brother obeying God and being blessed, he let another weed pop up - the weed of anger and murder. After he murdered his brother, he had the weed of stonewalling pop up. "Am I my brother's keeper?" he snarled at God. You can tell the beautiful Garden of Eden was already overgrown with weeds. The weed of murder is like the dandelion -hard to control. From the first murder up until today, the number would be in the trillions. Who would ever dream that the U.S., a nation started by Christian people, would approve of killing babies by the millions every year. Deceitfulness is a weed that also flourished from the beginning. By the time of the Babylonian captivity of Israel, the prophet Jeremiah could only bewail, *"The heart is deceitful above all things and desperately wicked."* It sounds like he was saying, "There is no hope." Years ago, the CEOs of big companies were considered honorable men. Today, it's common knowledge that many, maybe most of them, are scoundrels who try to deceive everybody.

For those who aren't sure of the names of some other common weeds, Paul gives a list in Romans 1:29-31. In Galatians 5:19-23, Paul takes this list and contrasts it with the good plants. The list of good plants should be memorized and then cultivated continually. When Jesus said, *"Watch and pray always that you may be accounted worthy,"* He was talking about keeping your garden clear of weeds. Some people think God will allow a few weeds in heaven. That's taking a big chance. Ephesians 5:27 plainly says the church should be holy and without blemish, not even a spot or wrinkle.

Learn to recognize weeds and kill them as soon as they appear. Let's just take one example. Someone criticizes you. Naturally, you resent it. You think of ways to repay - first the silent treatment, then a good chance comes to criticize him (or her), but hopefully, you have trained yourself to say every day, *"Let the words of my mouth and the meditation of my heart be pleasing in thy sight, O Lord."* So, you get convicted of thinking evil and you kill that weed by saying something kind instead. If you continue in this way, God will be pleased with you. *"So shall God open wide to you the gates of the eternal kingdom of our Lord and Savior, Jesus Christ."* (2 Peter 1:11)

## What A Christian Believes

There is only one true God and creator of the world, the one revealed in the Bible. God created Adam and Eve in His own likeness.

God is a Trinity: Father, Son, and Holy Spirit;
Man is also a trinity: body, soul, and spirit;
God as a spirit is invisible;

Man as spirit is also invisible;
God is only visible as Jesus;
Man is only visible as a body.

God gave man free will to do as he pleased with one law to keep as a test of his loyalty. He was given a stern warning that if he disobeyed, he would die.

Man broke the law and brought the curse of sin and death upon himself and all his descendants.

God immediately began a salvage operation by killing animals and clothing Adam and Eve with their skins. This showed them that sin caused death. They knew the animals died because of them.

God made His plan clear to them when it was time for them to bring a sin offering. Adam's son, Cain, brought of the fruit of the ground and was rejected. Abel, another son, brought a blood sacrifice and was accepted.

They were instructed to continue the blood sacrifices until Jesus, the Lamb of God, their Messiah, should come and lay His life down for them.

For thousands of years the Jews faithfully followed this plan and made sacrifices. Suddenly, without warning, the Messiah came and with mighty miracles proved His Deity. The Jewish leaders thought He was an impostor and rejected Him. This was in spite of the ultimate proof: His resurrection from the dead. Ironically the very day they were killing their sacrificial lambs, the leaders were taking Jesus, the true sacrifice, out to be crucified.

Tragically, the Jewish people followed their leaders and rejected their Messiah. Significantly, it wasn't too long after this that their sacrificial system was ended.

God's plan of salvation was now offered to all the world. Jesus first came to his own people, but they received Him not. However, He gave the many others who received him the power to become the sons of God (John 1:11 and 12). *"For God so loved the world that He gave His only begotten Son, that whosoever believes in Him should not perish, but have eternal life."* (John 3:16)

The most compelling reason for believing in Christ is the fulfillment of prophecy, thousands of them.

For example:
God would send a Messiah (Savior);
He would be rejected;
He would be killed;
He would be raised from the dead;
He would be received by the Gentiles as Savior;
The Romans would destroy Jerusalem;
The Jews would be scattered all over the world;
They would be persecuted everywhere.

Most importantly, they would be regathered to their homeland and become a nation again. This last happened in 1948. The Bible says that when the fig tree begins to bud, the end is near. The fig tree is Israel. In 1948, they came back to life. Think about it!!

## What a Waste!

It's good to learn early in life to avoid waste, but sad to say, it's a poorly understood concept. Billions of hours and billions of dollars are wasted every day. A whole library wouldn't even be big enough to show it. A newspaper told of the U. S. Congress voting millions of dollars for a bridge in Alaska that was going nowhere! Even that's not a drop in the bucket of what they waste. As they say, we get what we deserve.

Getting to more important matters, I visited prisons for years giving out life-changing literature and Bibles. The inmates now have lounges where they can socialize. The main activity, year in and year out, is card playing. What a waste!

Billions of people worship false gods; gods that tell them they will be reincarnated when they die into anything from an insect to a rich person, depending on how they followed their god's teaching. What a waste!

Billions of people believe in Allah, who teaches them to kill the infidels. Be a suicide bomber and go right to heaven to your own special harem. What a waste!

Billions of people worship entertainment; bigger arenas, bigger stadiums, more TV channels, and more Internet socializing. What a waste!

What about Christians? My guess is that plenty of Christians are wasting their time. This would include all those who have never been born again. Jesus said, "Except a man be born again, he cannot see the Kingdom of God." You can have your name on the roll, pay your dues, sing in the choir, etc., but following what the Lord says is the only thing that counts. Everything else is a waste. Another waste is the neglect of Bible study and prayer. This is the only resource available for Spiritual growth. Without it, we remain babies. (1 Peter 2:2) What a waste!

One more big waste is the effort to live a Christian life without the Holy Spirit. Jesus said in Matthew 5:48, "*Be ye perfect, even as your Father in heaven is perfect.*" Romans 7 describes Paul's Herculean effort to be perfect, to keep the law, and to live a righteous life. He gave up, saying it was impossible, but then in chapter 8 he gives the solution. "*There is no condemnation to them who walk not after the flesh but after the Spirit.*" In other words, be filled with God's Spirit and you can pass the test. Otherwise, you will fail and again, what a waste.

# What Kind of Shopper Are You?

I'm not a very good shopper, and when I accompany my wife to the store, the first thing I look for is a place to sit. Recently, I was doing just that and watching the shoppers go by with their overflowing carts. Every once in a while, there'd be a cart with just a few items. Well, I'm sure you know where I'm going with this, but you won't mind if I elucidate a little.

In my mind, I see a huge supermarket. It is named the "Marketplace of the World." This store sells everything imaginable, from the necessaries to pure trash. I'm watching these worldly people going by with their overloaded carts. I'm thinking they sure are enjoying the things of this world. There go the TV addicts with the new flat screen plasma sets. There go the teenagers loaded with designer clothes and sneakers. There go the hi-tech addicts with the latest electronic gear, etc., etc. Wait a minute, forgive me for being so keen eyed, but there goes Deacon Henry with a full cart. Wait another minute, there goes Pastor Bob. Am I seeing this right? Yes, it's all too true. Their carts are loaded. The worldly ones and the Christians are all together in this marketplace. Having the best of everything is the way to go.

I hear people saying these things aren't bad. They are necessary for the good life. But Paul says, *"Don't set your affections on things that are on earth for you are dead. - kill covetousness* (desire for things) *which is idolatry."* (Colossians 3:2-3 & 5) John says, *"Love not the world, neither the things that are in the world."* (1 John 2:15) Jesus said, *"Lay not up treasures on earth for where your treasure is, there will be your heart."* (Matthew 6:19 & 21)

I'm reminded of Esau, who sold his birthright for a bowl of stew. The stew was very good, but he lost his birthright. Jesus said, *"I counsel you to buy of me gold tried in the fire."* (Revelation 3:18) Your birthright is to walk with the Lord in this life and enjoy His heaven forever, but chances are, if you are so taken up with things in this world, you won't even think about the real gold. You could miss the greatest event of all history, the marriage supper of the Lamb. You only have one life and it will soon be past, only what's done for Christ will last.

Back to my observation of shoppers, I think I would rather be like the people with a couple of items in their cart, than like the great majority with carts overflowing.

## What You Know or Who You Know

"It's not what you know, it's who you know." That's what you hear when someone with doubtful intelligence lands a plum of a job. It is said with a bit of sarcasm. However, the saying is very apropos to the Christian. A person can have a ton of knowledge, and in the end, it's worthless. How many MD's and PhD's, etc., are there who have plenty of knowledge, but have never met the Lord.

Hosea 4:6 says, "*Without knowledge the people are destroyed,*" which sounds contradictory to the previous statement; however, he's talking about the knowledge of the Lord. That's the only kind of knowledge that counts. Anything else is temporary and worthless in the long run.

The Apostle Paul had his cup running over with knowledge. We can hardly understand all his teachings, but he said, "*O, that I might know Him,*" speaking of Jesus. Jesus said in John 17:3, "*This is eternal life, that they know You, the only true God, and Jesus Christ, whom You have sent* "

A very important caveat is in order. 'Knowing' has different meanings. You can know a fact, or a subject, like math, with the mind. You can also know a person with the mind. This kind of knowing is not Bible knowing. Paul said in Romans 10:9&10, "*If you believe in your heart -you shall be saved. For with the heart, man believes unto righteousness."* Jesus said in John 5:39, *"You search the scriptures, for you believe they give you eternal life, and the scriptures point to me. Yet you won't come to me so that I can give you eternal life."* This is a warning to all Bible readers: knowledge is not enough. The Jews knew the scriptures backward and forward, but they never took the time to cultivate a friendship with the Lord. They probably knew the 23rd Psalm by heart, but never thought of relating to the Lord as David did. They also probably knew Psalm 27:4 by heart, *"One thing I want from God, the thing I seek most of all is the privilege of meditating in His temple, living in His presence every day, delighting in His incomparable perfections and glory."* David had the true knowledge of God that saves.

## White Walls

In the dim past, when I was a boy, the tires on cars all had white walls. They seemed to dress up the cars and everyone tried to keep them clean. There was a special cleaning fluid to be sprayed on that was guaranteed to make your tires like new. But with all the efforts put out, it was hopeless. The tires were right down where the dirt was and there was just no way they could be kept clean. They were not dirty; they were dingy. Finally, someone said, "let's forget the white walls, and poof! The age of white walls was over.

Way back in the beginning of time, God created human souls, clean and pure. They fell into the mud, so to speak, and their souls got filthy dirty. This was very serious because filthy, in this case, means rebellion, and rebellion carries the death penalty. God, not willing to destroy his new creation, provided a sacrificial system whereby the filth could be put on an animal and the animal would then die in the place of the man. This kept them clean day-by-day, but to stay clean was impossible. It's a wonder God didn't say, "It's hopeless, let's forget it." He almost did when he decided to send a flood, but just in time, He found a man named Noah, who was trying, desperately to stay clean. God decided to start all over again with him. It didn't work too well, but God had a solution in mind.

He would, in due time, send His Son to take all the filth, plus the death penalty, upon Himself, and thus, free up man from his past. But that wasn't all. God knew that man, as a descendant of Adam, had a rebellious nature. Only one solution would work, and that was to replace his evil nature with a clean, pure nature. This was nothing less than providing His own Holy Spirit to dwell in man. Peter describes it this way, "*Repent,* (turn from sin) *every one of you, and be baptized in the name of Jesus Christ for the forgiveness of your sins and you shall receive the gift of the Holy Spirit.*" (Acts 2:38) "*He will give you through His great power, everything you need to live a truly good life - that you might be partakers of His divine nature, having escaped the corruption that is in the world.*" (2 Peter 1:3&4)

In the words of an old gospel song: "His power can make you what you ought to be. His blood can cleanse your heart and make you free. His love can fill your soul and you will see, 'twas best for Him to have His way in thee."

## Witnessing

Jesus said in Matthew 28:10, "*Go and teach all nations,*" in Mark 16:15, "*Go into all the world and preach the gospel.*" In Acts 1:8, "*You shall receive power after the Holy Ghost is come upon you and you shall be witnesses unto me.*" And in Luke 24:49, "*Tarry in Jerusalem until you be endued with power from on high.*" Since these words are the last instructions of Jesus to his disciples, and since they all bear on the same subject of witnessing, we have to believe this is the most important activity or function of the Kingdom of God in the gospel age.

For some reason or other, these verses have been brushed aside. Of course, we know Satan is behind it, but how was he able to make null and void the most important command of the Lord? My guess is that most people just don't want to witness, so preachers soft pedal it to extinction. In all other cases of commands being given, and people having to obey them, the results are just the opposite: most people do obey.

We know that all jobs are tied to a command structure. People know they must obey or lose their jobs. Soldiers, firemen, and policemen are trained in instant obedience. For example, if a house is on fire and there are people inside, a fireman must risk his life to get them out. If he doesn't have the courage to do it, he can't be a fireman. The same standards should apply to Christians. We believe that Satan has people in the palm of his hand. We know his purpose is to kill them. We know we should warn them. This is called witnessing, but we don't do it. The worst part of this scenario is that the consequences for the Christian are far worse than those in the natural world. To lose your job is bad, but to be reproved for failing to witness will be heartbreaking. It's true that the word 'witness' has different interpretations. Some say if you just live a good, honest life that is witnessing. Trouble is, unbelievers often live better than Christians. Some say going to church is a witness. Trouble is, half the people that go to church are nominal Christians (in name only). For an example of true witnessing, read the early chapters of the Book of Acts.

In another aspect of the case, Jesus said, "*I will make you fishers of men.*" Every fisherman takes fishing gear with him. If he goes without gear, you know something is wrong. Every Christian is called to be a witness. If he goes out of the house, it's a witnessing trip. If he forgets his gear (tracts, etc.), something is wrong. We see what's wrong when we look at two words preceding the making of fishers of men. They are, "Follow me." This should give every Christian pause. Could it be that we're not witnessing because we're not followers? It's something to think about.

One of the worst decisions the early church leaders made was to divide the people into clergy and laity. When Jesus said, "*I ordain you that you should bring forth fruit,*" He was talking to all Christians. When He said, "*You shall be witnesses unto me,*" He meant all of us. (John 15:16) When Peter said, "*You are a royal priesthood,*" he meant all of us. The one hundred and twenty people filled with the Holy Spirit on the Day of Pentecost were ordinary people; fishermen, tax collectors, etc. Because of this division of the people by the early leaders, the great majority of Christian people say witnessing is the preacher's job.

The Bible has a strong word for those who neglect to witness. Ezekiel 3:17 says, "*If you refuse to warn the wicked, they will die in their sins, but I will demand your blood for theirs. If you warn him and he repents, he shall live and you have saved your own life, too.*" On the positive side, Daniel 12:3 says, "*They that turn many to righteousness shall shine as the stars forever.*" Proverbs 11:30 says, "*He that wins souls is wise.*"

## Word of God

John 1:1, "*In the beginning was the Word and the Word was - God.*" Jesus is here called the Word and the Word is called Jesus. They are interchangeable. They are one and the same. It is the same as with us. I am my word and my word is me. If you want to know me, you have to hear my words and if you hear my words, you know me. Right here we see how important it is to get into the Word. If we say we want more of Jesus in our lives, it follows that the only way for this to happen is to get into the Word, knowing that the Word is Jesus.

John 1:11-12 says Jesus came into the world but the world didn't want Him. Those that did want Him were transferred from Satan's family into God's family. Jesus calls this being born again (John 3:3). Salvation is like the birth process. Now everyone knows that immediately upon being born, a baby is hungry. It instinctively craves milk and when we're born again, we will crave the Word. The Bible says in 1 Peter 2:2 that "*As newborn babes, desire the milk of the Word that you may grow.*" It follows that if you have no desire for the Word, you just weren't born. This is the litmus test, absolutely reliable. We know from John 1:12 that we are born again by receiving Christ by faith. This is explained further in the parable of the sower. (Matthew

13) Jesus tells of seeds being sown in different kinds of soil and only the good soil produces fruit. Then He explains in verse 23 that the seed is the Word and the good soil is the person who receives the Word and understands it. In other words, you get into the Word and the Word gets into you. This is just a start.

Psalm 1 says a good person will stay in the Word. He will meditate on the Word day and night and he'll be like a tree bringing forth fruit. This verse indicates that the Word is not only necessary for the new birth, but it is absolutely necessary for continued growth. Jesus said, *"Man does not live by bread alone but by every Word of God."* (Luke 4:14) He said, *"If you continue in my Word, you shall know the truth and the truth shall set you free."* (John 8:31) Jesus said, *"The words I speak are spirit and life."* (John 6:63) This is exactly what we need and there's no other way to get it except by reading the Word. As we continue in the Word, we see that God is looking for growth and development unto maturity. Paul says in 1 Corinthians 3:2, *"I have fed you with milk* (elementary lessons) *and not with meat* (deeper truth) *for you were not able to bear it."* In other words, these people didn't stay in the Word long enough to grow out of babyhood, and Paul was disappointed with them.

Hebrews 4:12 gives an example of what the meat is, *"The Word is alive and powerful able to divide soul and spirit."* Here you need to know that the soul (flesh self) is the seat of sin. The Word does the necessary job of separating soul from the spirit. The soul life leads to death. The spiritual life leads to heaven. This is made clear in Romans chapter 8, which is very strong meat. Hebrews 5:14 says strong meat belongs to them that are mature. How does one get mature? Only by getting into the strong meat.

God's ultimate purpose is that we be conformed to the image of His Son, Jesus. (Romans 8:29) This can only be done by *"walking not in the flesh but in the Spirit* (in the Word)." (Romans 8:4) Colossians 3:16 says, *"Let the Word of God dwell in you richly."* Psalm 1 says, *"Meditate day and night."* John 17:17 says, *"Sanctify them* (make them perfect) *through your truth. Your Word is truth.*" Finally, brethren, as Paul says so many times, take the sword of the Spirit, which is the Word of God, and begin to use it as Jesus did in Matthew 4:1-10. Just keep saying, "It is written," and the victory is yours.

## Writing Articles

For a person who struggled mightily in college to get a theme written every week, and who hoped desperately to at least get a C, this article is a 180° turn around. I say with the Amish, "Lord, why am I so soon old and so late smart?"

As you have surmised, this article is about the art of writing articles, at least how it started with me. I've had the conviction for some time, that I, as well as all Christians, should be able to expound on most Bible subjects. Peter said we should be ready always to give an answer to anybody that asks a reason for the hope we have. (1 Peter 3:15)

So, I've dabbled in writing over the years, but just for my own amusement or amazement. The Titanic film changed all that. The film was very moving, of course, and I couldn't help but think about it. I began writing my thoughts. They seemed to flow very smoothly from one aspect to another, without any effort. I was truly amazed and took it that the Lord was doing it. It reminded me of Jesus' words, *"The water I give shall be in you, a well of water springing up into everlasting life."* (John 4:14) John 7:38 says, *"Out of his innermost being shall flow rivers of living water."* You may say I don't seem to have any living water. I said that too, but I discovered something. The more you get into the Word, which is the living water, the more it wants to flow out. You know about the Sea of Galilee, how it flows to the Dead Sea. Everywhere it flows, there's life and much fruit. But, when it flows into the Dead Sea, it stops and that's the end of life and fruit. The thought occurs to me that writing articles could be the same as prophecy, where you write instead of speak. (Acts 2:4) This could be one way to obey God's command, *"Covet to prophesy."* (1 Corinthians 14:39) I found myself doing just that, coveting more nuggets of truth and they kept coming and I praise the Lord for it. Then I had a new thought. Instead of throwing my nuggets into the drawer, I should make copies and give them out. The Bible says, *"A good man* (woman) *out of the good treasure of his heart brings forth good things."* (Matthew 12:35) I had some good things, but what good were they stashed in a drawer?

Now the point of this article is to encourage you to write. You might say there are too many articles already. Every magazine is full of them. This is true, but no one sees things the way you do. We're all unique and it might just be, that what you write is the cup of water that some thirsty soul needs. It can be very rewarding. I gave out a couple of my articles to a mechanic in Pep Boys and later he told me one of them was the answer to a big problem he had. So, pick some topic you're interested in and start writing. The first two or three sentences actually become like the primer of the pump. As you write thoughts come crowding in, thoughts that hadn't even occurred to you before. This, you might say is going out on a limb - by faith. Like Abraham, you're not sure where you're going but you know He's your guide. God wants us to be streams in the desert. Psalm 46:4 says, *"There is a river that makes glad the City of God."* Ezekiel 47:9 says, *"Everywhere the river goes, there is healing."* Does God want us to write things down? *"Write the vision, make it plain,"* (Hebrews 2:2) *"Write the words I have spoken."* (Jeremiah 30:2) *"The words I command - write on the posts of your house and on your gates."* (Deuteronomy 6:9) *"Daniel wrote the dream and told the sum of it."* (Daniel 7:1) For a little caveat, don't get discouraged. Most people you give your articles to will chuck them. Just remember, you're in good company. More people chuck the Bible than read it.

But God says, *"My Word shall not return to me void, but will accomplish that which I please."* (Isaiah 55:11) Like the Pep Boys' man, you don't know what God might do with one of your articles. Look what Paul said about the Corinthians, *"In everything you are enriched by Him in all utterance and in all knowledge,"* and I add, in all writing. They were definitely sharing, or Paul couldn't have said that.

I was reading a book by J. P. Caussade called, "Abandoned to God's Providence." It was a real gem of a book. I was surprised to learn that it was made up of letters that someone had saved. Someone else discovered them, and Christians had a book full of spiritual meat. No one starts writing what he thinks will be a classic. It just happens. In the Christian world, it is writing as led by the Holy Spirit. In speaking of the scriptures, Peter said, *"Holy men of God spoke* (wrote) *as they were moved by the Holy Ghost."* (2 Peter 1:21) Paul said, *"All scripture is given by inspiration of God."* (2 Timothy 3:16) This should be the intention and the resolve of all Christian writers.

Made in the USA
Middletown, DE
08 November 2021